The Good
News According
to Luke

RICHARD ROHR

The Good News According to Luke

Spiritual Reflections

A Crossroad Book
The Crossroad Publishing Company
New York

The Crossroad Publishing Company
www.CrossroadPublishing.com

Printed in the United States of America

.**Library of Congress Cataloging-in-Publication Data**

Rohr, Richard.
    The good news according to Luke / Richard Rohr.
      p. cm.
    ISBN 0-8245-1490-4; ISBN 0-8245-1966-3 (pbk.)
     1. Bible. N.T. Luke – Criticism, interpretation, etc. I. Title.
BS2595.2.R64   1997
226.4'07–dc21   97-753

Contents

Preface

When I see how people sometimes distort and misuse the Bible, I wonder why God bothered to give it to us. The Scripture was meant to be a testimony of God's efforts at liberating and uniting humanity, but instead we continue to interpret it for our own purposes, even to hate, oppress, and divide God's creation. The corruption of the best is always the worst.

I get angry with humans manipulating the Bible for personal and political purposes, and I also get frustrated with God for letting it happen century after century. Lord, couldn't you have made it easier? Couldn't you have given us a Bible that couldn't be misused? Couldn't you have given us your message clearly and orderly like our Constitution? You know, Point one. Point two. Do this. Don't do that?

But God didn't choose to do it that way. The Bible seems to be a "text in travail," revealing the answers more through the problems — the process itself — than through clear conclusions.

Since the divine agenda seems to be quite different from ours, it might be wise to lay some groundwork for understanding Luke by asking some basic questions about faith and revelation: What is God trying to do in the world through the sacred Scriptures? What is happening in this faith chronicle called the Bible?

At this point in human history, the issues are so urgent and demanding that we cannot waste any more time flirting with the Bible. We are ready for an adult relationship with a very mature partner.

Acknowledgments

I would especially like to thank Louis Savary, who has had the humility, love, and patience to move this text from spoken word on tape to written and readable form.

His work was refined and supported by John Eagleson and the family-like staff at Crossroad. With such friends as these, work is turned into joy and my rambling thoughts become words that even Luke might be proud of.

One

A Perspective on Luke's Gospel

All religions have tried to discover something about God's nature and purpose. They have used their own common sense, their own logic, their own experience and their own images to come up with a description of God. What is unique about the Judeo-Christian tradition is that we believe God is the one who has revealed to us who God is. It is much more the story of God trying to get to us. This revelation came through the faith experience of the Jewish people, of which Christianity is a development. We believe God has chosen the path of divine self-revelation. God is the one who told us about God. God has shared with us what goes on in the divine heart. In addition, Christians believe that God has even shared with us the "divine flesh" in Jesus. The bottom line is: God has revealed Godself to us through *self-disclosure.*

People, especially in Western civilization, are uncomfortable with personal and intimate self-revelation coming from God — or from anyone else, for that matter. We're more comfortable thinking about God conceptually than standing in the powerful presence of God's self-revelation. A cartoon made this point well. There were pictured two doorways, one marked "Heaven" and the other marked "Lecture on Heaven." Waiting to enter the lecture room was a long line of people, but almost no one stood before the door leading to the direct experience of God.

Since we are more comfortable in our heads than in our hearts, we tend to avoid facing God's self-disclosure in Scripture. Instead of viewing the Bible as a personal and intimate dialogue between God and

humans — characterized by divine revelation and our human faith response to it — we have turned Scripture largely into conceptual and
informational content: a set of facts, figures, data, and phenomena
which we are supposed to learn. As long as we learn these facts and
ideas, we believe that somehow they will save us, liberate us, and
bring us to God. We have squeezed the biblical story of God's self-
revelation into an intellectual package — a document of conceptual
material.

Thus, we have transformed the Bible into an abstraction. Once
such a transformation happens and people agree to it, we begin to
argue about the interpretations of that abstraction. We prefer to argue
about the Bible and how it is to be interpreted, because the content
has become the all-important thing.

We seem to believe that God could create human unity, bring about
the divine purposes, and reveal God's heart through words and doctrinal formulations. But the most precise formulation of words and
their most accurate translations into other languages can never communicate the heart of God and the mind of Christ. Still, we are more
comfortable with words, formulations, translations, and arguments.
We prefer the lecture on heaven to heaven itself.

I won't say that biblical information isn't important; however, during the past four or five hundred years, scriptural facts and figures
have been so emphasized that the Bible has become a tool for dividing
people rather than uniting them. Throughout history, we see groups
taking sides because of the Bible.

The Bible is not a lecture or treatise on God; it is a story of the
experience of God. It is the story of God revealing Godself to a people
and what happens after that encounter: some run away from it, some
avoid it, some dismiss it, some actively oppose it, some waver, and
some fall to their knees in recognition. It is always a text in travail,
never just easy answers like "the seven secrets of success."

It's been said that Protestantism has usually depended on scriptural authority, while Catholicism depended on both Scripture and
tradition. "Tradition" is an ambiguous word. For many people it just
means "the way we used to do things." Most who call themselves tra-
ditionalists are simply conservatives by temperament. It scares many
Protestant brothers and sisters when Catholics claim that any way we
used to do things is always good to draw upon.

When I use the word "tradition," I'm talking about one continuous four-thousand-year tradition — that is, two thousand years of Judaism and two thousand years of Christianity — not about traditions, plural. Traditions, as endearing as they might be, can also become clannish, violent, xenophobic, and resistant to true transcendence.

Tradition is what gives breadth to a Catholic theology; it draws not only from the chronicled accounts we find in the biblical books, but also from the ongoing events of the believing community. Tradition says, in effect, that God is continuously revealing the divinity. God's self-revelation may be found not only in the sacred books, but also in the people who live in the spirit of God in every age — and in the history of our planet and all creation.

I think the importance of tradition in this sense is justified in terms of what we see Luke doing in his gospel. Luke himself is creating his gospel by using Scripture and tradition, and he's doing it within a believing community. In putting together his gospel, he's not only drawing on past Scriptures, such as the Hebrew Bible and Mark's Gospel, but he's also weaving in contemporary spirituality, knowledge of the theological schools of Judaism, experience of the times, insights of the believing community (the living Body of Christ), and putting it all together.

If you insist that it's not "biblical" to integrate Scripture and tradition in the context of the believing community, logically you must also assert that the New Testament writers were not biblical. If the only way to be biblical is to quote the Scriptures and nothing else, then the evangelists themselves were not biblical, because they didn't just quote the Scriptures. The early Christians used the Scriptures as part of an entire way of thinking, relating, and communicating within their faith community. As communicators of a message and a meaning, the evangelists called upon the best they could gather from their tradition as a faith community to communicate God's power and presence.

This approach seems to me to be so self-evident it is amazing that certain people who claim to be biblical don't see it. By their definition of biblical, the very biblical people they quote are not biblical. This is important because, even today, to hold such a narrow definition of biblical — "If it isn't in the Bible, it isn't true" — is to severely limit reality.

Thus, Catholicism has for its authority the book, tradition, and the believing community (the Body of Christ). For me, these three sources are all summed up in the word "church."

The Bible as a Faith Community's Story

Christian Scripture remains a point of contention and division because it is interpreted apart from the living church to which it was first given, apart from the various early Christian communities each telling its story of their experience of the risen Christ. The New Testament indeed contains divine words about Christ, but mostly it contains words spoken by the early faith community as it stood in relation to Christ. The Bible's words reflect the way Christ was understood by the men and women who made up the church when Matthew, Mark, Luke, John, Paul, and the others were writing.

The sacred text, then, is one step removed from a direct experience of Christ. It is now generally accepted by Scripture scholars that most of the evangelists — certainly Mark and Luke — never physically encountered Jesus. Matthew and John, as gospel authors, were traditionally seen as apostles, but Mark and Luke weren't. They, like us, knew him in the context of a believing community. Luke perhaps knew Jesus through Paul, but Paul never knew Jesus in the flesh either. Paul learned about Jesus through the early faith communities, those living bodies of Christ whom he visited and lived with. It was the same for Luke; he learned to know Jesus by living as part of a first-century Christian faith community.

When scholars refer to a Christian community in the early church they are not talking about anything comparable to today's big-city parishes. Very likely we're talking about gatherings of thirty or forty people, very small, but amazingly influential groups of people. They were able to touch significant numbers of people and change the course of history because of their conviction and commitment to each other.

As a group of believers grows larger and larger, a kind of anonymity and noncommitment emerges. We all know that experience in our large American parishes. The contemporary church is trying, especially in the Third World, to allow base communities to reemerge, but it will be many years before they really take hold in America. As long as we have the priesthood running everything in big parishes, we won't feel the need for smaller core groups (or cells) in Christianity.

We know that in the beginnings of the church, Christians experienced the faith in cells, or small communities, out of which came a great deal of conviction and commitment to each other. Luke reflects this high degree of commitment. The questions he deals with in his gospel are very pastoral and interpersonal, nonacademic. They are questions about their relationship with Jesus and with his Body, that is, each other.

Scholars suggest Luke's is the third written gospel, following Mark and Matthew, but before John. There is a tendency to place Luke's Gospel later than Mark and Matthew — around the year 85 — because of the amount of theological development it contains. Many well-developed theological themes are found in Luke, certainly many more than in Mark, where the message is still simple and direct, probably because it was written perhaps twenty years previously.

To get Luke's chronological perspective, imagine that it is 1980. Most people in 1980 do not remember 1933 very clearly. I don't. I wasn't born then. (I suspect Luke was like me, not even born when the key events happened.) Let's say there was an outstanding itinerant preacher who traveled around Canada between 1930 and 1933 but his story hasn't been written. In 1980, his story is still waiting to be written, and I have been asked to write it.

That's the perspective Luke faced, that almost fifty-year stretch between the death and resurrection of Jesus until the year 80, including all those intervening decades — the 30s, 40s, 50s, 60s, and 70s — while the tradition of the Jesus experience was being mulled over, shared, and passed on by his followers. Certain stories are being selected for telling over and over; others are being forgotten. This almost fifty-year period shaped what we call the "oral tradition." Finally, after a generation or more of believers had come and gone, sometime around the year 80, Luke started putting together the elements of his gospel story.

From this perspective, the resurrection is not the end of Luke's Gospel but its beginning. If the gospel is a recording of the faith experience being shared among groups of Christian people during the first century, then Jesus' resurrection marks the start of their faith journey. Sometime around the year 33 C.E., their experience of the risen Jesus finally gave birth to the church. From within that faith community trying to continue to live their belief in the risen Jesus, the gospels were created.

This perspective is not understood by most people who use the Bible; they don't deal with those first fifty years of the church's experience. Rather, they pretend that the Christian Scriptures came straight down from heaven in the form of divine dictation. Some naively think God spoke the gospel's words into the evangelists' ears. That understanding gives the Scriptures an authority unrelated to culture and history and, unfortunately, unrelated to reality as well.

What is written in the biblical text describes the reflection of the believing community — what I call the church — upon the mystery of Jesus. What is written in Luke's Gospel describes a believing community's reflection on the mystery of the risen Lord at the time Luke was writing, reflecting their questions, problems, and needs. I am not denying that this sacred text is the word of the Lord, but it is more accurate to say the Bible contains the messages of God as they are received, understood, prayed upon, and used to lead a community of believers.

Those who passed on the oral tradition and those who put the Christ story into written books were real people, like you and me, walking among a community of fellow believers. When they began writing, they had already been gathering from the tradition what would be helpful for their situation in answering the questions believers had about God's revelation and the problems they faced in relating to the risen Lord and to each other. Luke was writing his version of the good news for his own people in the 80s, who were facing their own particular problems and questions.

For example, one big problem Luke's community seemed to be facing was much the same worry or anxiety that Mark's community felt. Many were still presuming, as Jesus himself seems to have done, that the Second Coming — the Parousia — was imminent. No one denied, including Luke, that Jesus had said, *"I tell you truly, there are some standing here who will not taste death before they see the kingdom of God"* (9:27) and *"I tell you solemnly, before this generation has passed away all will have taken place"* (21:32).

If Luke knew the Parousia was no longer imminent, why would Luke in his gospel text repeat Jesus' inaccurate prediction? In these passages, Luke is perhaps showing us some thoughts and predictions from Jesus' human consciousness which in fact did not work out. Perhaps that's one of the reasons Luke asserts that Jesus' mind grew in wisdom, age, and grace (see 2:40, 52).

To accept that something Jesus said didn't actually happen on schedule is a new way of thinking for most Christians today, but the facts are quite evident. Jesus — at least as Luke presents him — does not always have correct historical and geographical information, and here Luke shows that Jesus does not have a clear understanding of the way history is going to unfold. To Luke, it seems acceptable that Jesus is operating out of a fallible human consciousness. That's in no way to deny his divinity. It really makes more overwhelming the mystery of the incarnation, that the one whom we would later call the Second Person of the Blessed Trinity and the Son of God entered into our humanity so fully. Luke is showing us that Jesus really entered into our clouded human consciousness, taking on all its limitations.

At this point in the last quarter of the first century, Christian communities had become aware that either Christ was delaying his return, or it wasn't going to happen the way they thought it would and the way Jesus said it would. To us, two thousand years later, the fact that the risen Lord didn't come back in glory during the first generation hasn't been a problem. Unlike the early church, we weren't told in catechism classes that Jesus was going to return in our lifetime. But that first generation of Christians were taught that and believed it.

That's why there's such an emphasis on it in Mark's Gospel. He's calling his community to radical total discipleship because, apparently, Mark believed, "All we have is a few short years left, and the game's over." (This is, of course, always true for all of us!)

It's interesting that Luke is also an evangelist of radical discipleship, but he's changed the wording and the understanding. He's not making the call softer, but in telling us that we must take up our cross, he adds the word "daily" (9:23). In other words. Luke says it looks like it's going to be conversion, day after day, for the rest of our lives. It won't be just one big dramatic "leave all things and follow me." He's saying, "It's going to be a long haul."

Luke is speaking from a different perspective. People in his community are becoming aware that it looks like Jesus isn't going to return any time soon. Things are not going to happen as earlier Christians had expected. Luke's Gospel is in many ways trying to help his community deal with that traumatic awareness and show them how to experience the presence of the risen Lord and deepen their common faith through "ordinary time."

Until we understand that the gospel writers were each responding to the needs of their generation and their community, we inevitably *misuse* the Bible for our own purposes (using texts out of context) instead of *using* it positively as Luke did (using old texts to reveal pat-

terns in a new context). For example, many today misuse the Bible as
a private source-text for their own spiritual enrichment or to find their
own specific answers to life's problems. That's the way the majority of
the world treats the Bible, but I don't think that's what the gospel is
about. That's not what God intended nor what Luke intended.

Rather than give us concrete solutions to personal problems, the
Bible's grand vision offers us a context in which we will indeed find
our answers, but first we need to be aligned with the larger vision-
pattern-direction. Great religion resituates us in a coherent universe
of meaning, and out of that come the answers. The point of studying the Bible is not simply to have memorized Luke's Gospel or to be
able to recite dozens of quotes from its pages. The important thing is
that Christ lives now, and in relating to the risen Christ in a believing
community we are discovering our own version of the good news, our
own universe of meaning. It is the old text empowering a new text by
revealing the universal and common context.

Western religions characteristically retreat into the past, celebrate
the past, and promote consciousness of the past. That's one reason
Christianity has become known as a conservative religion. As a group,
we Christians love the status quo, like to argue about the past, and are
fixated on historical facts. Typically, our primary biblical focus is not
on the experience of the risen Lord of Luke's faith community, but on
"what really happened back there." Like news reporters, we want to
know "the facts." We expect Luke is telling us about the good old days
when Jesus walked this earth and people saw him, because we're most
curious about "what really happened." But I'm saying "what really
happened" is simply not the important question for us. It certainly
wasn't for Luke.

Suppose someone had made a live videotape of Jesus, which we
could play and be certain he really existed and really made this or
that statement. Knowing the facts about Jesus would not solve the
faith problem. The question of faith would still remain. Even with a
credible videotape of Jesus, we would still sit around and argue about
what he really meant when he said this or that.

Many today are convinced that the facts of Jesus' life are the important issue; they want to settle once and for all that the Jesus event really
happened and that it really happened in a certain way. Such information doesn't — and cannot — answer the question of faith. It seems
so obvious to me that no amount of facts and information could ever

answer the question of faith, yet people who quote the Bible use the Scriptures in this way consistently. They confuse faith with facts, and in so doing miss the major invitation of divine revelation. Revelation is telling us about the patterns that are always true, the patterns that connected all things then and still do so now. When we become too preoccupied with *then,* we tend to miss that revelation is also happening *now.* Then and now are two very different lenses. We will be using the lens of *then,* as Luke did, so that we can discover the lens of *now.*

Divine Revelation and the Faith of Jesus

Divine revelation is the self-communication of God to humans. It is God disclosing Godself to us, telling us in the most revealing way who God is. I believe God has always been doing this self-disclosure. God has never stopped giving and revealing Godself to us. In this revelation process, God is both the giver and the given.

God's first self-revelation to us is creation itself, the beauty of this world. The more I travel, the more I am overwhelmed by the beauty and glory of this planet and the intricacies of nature. Creation is God's continuous self-disclosure, a divine revelation going on since the beginning of time and continuing until the end of time. Those who have eyes to see can recognize the touch of God everywhere. Seeing God's self-revelation in creation is largely a matter of how we look at it. Most of us need to be taught by the Spirit how to see with "the eyes of God."

I presume that you, my readers, approach the gospels with the eyes of faith, not simply as reporters and scholars asking factual and academic questions. My main interests are the faith questions, only secondarily the factual and academic ones. I also presume you are exploring the Scriptures in a faith community, leading you to ask questions like: How can we live and love in the Lord? How can we be life-giving in our homes, communities, workplaces? I also hope it's your heart that's searching, and not simply your intellect looking for answers: "In what year did this event take place? How did that miracle happen? What does this word really mean in the original Greek?"

In his book *Discipleship,* Juan Carlos Ortiz caricatures biblical scholars preoccupied with etymologies by creating the following scenario: Suppose I wrote you a letter which began, "Dear Agnes. How are you?" and continued on telling you about my current life for the rest of the letter. As you read my letter, instead of picturing me talking to you as a friend, you took each word and analyzed it. For example, you would say to yourself as you read, "Dear" is an Anglo-Saxon word denoting affectionate relationship, and "Agnes" comes from a Latin word meaning "lamb." Next, you would analyze the grammar and structure of each sentence, categorizing each phrase as colloquial or classical, essential or parenthetical. And so on.

First, I wouldn't want anybody to analyze my personal letters like that; second, such analysis would not help them get to know me better or understand my meaning more deeply. And yet we do exactly that with Paul's letters. We pull the chapters apart and analyze each verse; we're sure some important meaning is hidden between the second and third sentences, and we're sure that a really smart person who's studied Greek can find the hidden meaning, but all of us dumb beginners will never understand it.

That's one way the Scriptures are commonly misused. The Lord never intended the Bible to have such distorted authority. I'm not a demographer, but I would guess that about 90 percent of the people who ever walked on this planet couldn't read. Given that fact, do you think God would make divine self-revelation completely dependent on a certain level of academic education? I don't think so.

I was trained to be a Bible teacher. What I am going to do in this book is offer you a love for the Scriptures and a faith approach to them that is still intellectually satisfying. I believe with all my heart in the true authority of the Scriptures; I do not want to offer a false authority that blinds instead of enlightens and divides reality instead of revealing the patterns that unite all humanity.

Divine revelation means God reveals God. God is communicating Godself to us, and the divine communication is everywhere evident in creation, even before the writing of the Scriptures. It has always been evident for those who can see. That's how Abraham knew God, even though he never had the Bible. Abraham knew how to see.

How did Abraham manage to know God? Abraham knew God by the relationship called "faith." Faith is the other side of the coin of revelation. Faith is revelation received and responded to. An act of faith is a *response to a disclosure*. Faith is meant to be an ongoing dialogue of divine disclosure and human response, an ever deeper divine disclosure and an ever deeper human response. Just like any love affair.

In contrast, many have a faith that is a reaching out and grasping for God, but is not really a response to God's revelation. Such people are responding to their own needs, fears, or desires — to anything but God's self-revelation — and this can easily lead to a distorted understanding of God. When faith is not based on God's personal self-disclosure, it generates a religion which is mostly wishful thinking, projection, and legalism, since such religion is, for the most part, a product of people's own creation, their own needs, and their own desires projected onto God.

In the best moments of the Judeo-Christian tradition, God was disclosing God to humanity and humanity was listening, welcoming, praying, and receiving the divine revelation, then responding to it with a full heart. Holistic, deep, and rich faith is a whole-hearted response to God's self-revelation.

Much faith experience today fails to be a response to divine revelation, because responsive faith requires *the listening life,* a life that waits attentively and that is not quick to judge or to dissect the word of God. That is why prayer and the contemplative life are necessary to understand what is happening in the Judeo-Christian faith tradition.

We can also call divine revelation — this self-disclosure of God — the "Word of God." But where is the Word of God really found? For Christians, the Word of God is summed up and encapsulated in Jesus Christ, even though it was already and is now spread out through all creation and all history.

Jesus is called the Word of God because the human self-consciousness of Jesus, his growing self-awareness, is the focus and locus of divine revelation fully welcomed. Since the Word of God is Jesus himself, the divine self-communication is understood perfectly only in the mind and self-awareness of Jesus. We believe that as Son of the Father Jesus received perfectly what the Father was saying. He did not reject it, fight it, dissect it, misunderstand it, or misuse it. The human self-consciousness of Jesus is the walking Bible, the living Bible. This perspective on Scripture is very important to grasp.

The study of Luke's Gospel faces that very important question of the self-consciousness of Jesus. Many are afraid to deal with this question; it scares them to think that Jesus might have grown in his self-knowledge, that maybe Jesus lying in the manger didn't know everything, that maybe Jesus at age twelve didn't know everything, and in fact that maybe Jesus nailed to the cross didn't know everything.

Already in the first Christian centuries, two heresies were condemned by early church councils. One was the Monophysite heresy; the other was called Arianism. "Monophysite" comes from two Greek words: *mono* meaning "one" and *physis* meaning "nature." The Monophysites were a group in the church who believed Jesus possessed only one nature, a divine nature; that, in fact, Jesus was not a human being at all but only a divine being in disguise, walking around pretending to be man. The church said Monophysitism was false, since Christ is totally human and totally divine. Unfortunately, the church fathers didn't explain how Christ could be both totally human and totally divine. All they said was it was a mystery and only the Holy Spirit could help us make sense out of it.

The other heresy, called Arianism, is named after Arias, its primary proponent. Arias said, in effect, that Jesus was totally human and not divine at all. Most contemporary Western thinkers, including some in the church, might be classified as Arian, believing that Jesus was a good man and a great teacher, but not God.

On the other hand, most Christians have been and continue to be Monophysites, in the sense that they do not believe Jesus was totally human. These are people scandalized at and unready to accept the idea that Jesus grew in his self-knowledge, that Jesus as a child did not know everything. They refuse to believe that Jesus developed just as you and I do. Luke says of Jesus: *"He grew in wisdom, age, and grace before God and others"* (2:52). That statement upsets them, because their faith is based on a false revelation in which Jesus is largely an idol, that is, God *pretending* to live in a human body. For them, Jesus walked around the earth displaying divine knowledge unknown from all eternity; consequently, those who really listen to his wisdom and really understand it have a perfect "in" to God. Neither do these same people believe that Jesus indeed submitted himself to the flesh, that he chose the way of the incarnation, and that, for Jesus, the human condition — the human body, human consciousness, and the human faith struggle — characterize his own life journey and his way of communicating the divine to us.

In simple terms, the medium is the message, process is the context, and there must be a coherence between means and ends. Without such integral teaching, we end up with Christian absurdities such as enforced baptism, killing for peace, hating the material world, fleeing to "spirituality." By holding together the whole process, Jesus *became* the message, a living synthesis of *how to do it*. He *is* the message more than just being the messenger. He said, "Follow me" more than "Believe me."

Jesus as Model for Living a Life of Faith

Jesus presents to us his own human life — walking the earth just as you and I walk it — as the model for living a life of faith, that is, a life continually responding to God's self-revelation.

Jesus' own faith journey is our teaching; it is the word of God for us. That's why we call him the Word of God. It's not that Jesus was walking around with all knowledge in his mind and doling it out to us and that made him the Word of God; rather, Jesus was growing in his own understanding of faith and of the kingdom. Jesus' growing process is, in fact, the best teaching for us.

Let's make a human comparison. Suppose a superstar of knowledge moves into your house as a boarder. With three Ph.D.'s after his name, he sits at your supper table each evening dispensing information about nuclear physics, cyberspace, and psychoneuroimmunology and giving ultimate answers to every question you ask. However, he doesn't lead you through his thinking process or even involve you in it; he simply gives out conclusions he has reached. (I'm sure you know some people like this.) You might find his conclusions interesting and even very helpful; but the way he relates to you will not set you free, empower you, or make you feel good about yourself. His wisdom will not liberate you, it will not invite you to growth and life; indeed, it will in the end make you feel inferior and dependent. Now that's exactly the way we have used Jesus. We have treated him like a person with five Ph.D.'s coming to tell us his conclusions.

We humans don't really want conclusions. Do you know what we want? We want to experience the process. We want someone to walk with us through all the stages of faith; we want someone to hold our hand, to love us, to support us, and to believe in us while we are in process. You and I are always in process; that's where we live our lives; that's what interests us. Even our faith is in process. The fact is we're really not all that concerned about having perfect conclusions. We need someone to help us make sense out of the journey itself.

G. K. Chesterton once said, "Certainly the truth is very important but I am not so preoccupied with the truth. I'm more preoccupied with the interesting." The "interesting" is what preoccupies us all. If the interesting is also the truth, so much the better. We want the truth, and Jesus is concerned that we discover it for ourselves. But he does it by walking with us, like a brother, on our daily journeys.

That's the pattern of the incarnation: that Jesus came neither to be the Answer Man nor the Conclusion Man, but to walk with us in his ongoing self-discovery. Actually, he is an Answer Man for us when we grasp his life in its totality. His Father at the end transformed all his crucifixions into life. In this sense, he is a Conclusion Man for us, too. But that's not the key point. The absolutely important thing is that someone walk with us now and help us to connect the dots. Jesus is the pattern that connects and the image that redeems our disconnected lives — even the dots that feel like failure.

Now that's a very different use of the Scriptures and the word of God, but I do believe you might want to call such an experience "salvation" and such a person your "Savior."

The mortal, historical Jesus — if you want to use those terms — did not found a church. It would be fair to say that in his human lifetime Jesus probably had no idea that this Christian history, including the church as we know it today, was going to happen. (Again, that assertion may be very shocking to some people.) Certainly, the human, historical Jesus never heard of or conceived of the Roman Catholic Church. The church we know in this century didn't exist in the human mind of Jesus.

Does that mean the church is unreal or false? Of course not. The human Jesus was simply not dealing with a lot of the questions you and I deal with. It was his mission on earth to wrestle with a handful of basic questions about the nature of God, the nature of reality, and the nature of the good. In effect, he tells the Twelve, "Get your basic assumptions right about what's happening between God and humanity — that goodness is at work, that God is faithful, and that humans are images of God. If you understand these things and you create a life together in community, you'll find your own answers to the issues you face."

The problem begins when a people disagree with each other on basic assumptions. For example, many believe the human person at core is bad and evil. If we're going to go forward together creating a faith community, we have to work out agreement on fundamental as-

sumptions. This lack of basic alignment is a central problem blocking genuine church renewal today. Others debate how many basic assumptions are needed. For me, they are the same ones Jesus addressed: God and humanity in relationship as well as the meaning of life, love, justice, and freedom.

So if the mortal, historical Jesus did not found the church, who did? The Risen Christ founded the church. That's why I say the gospels don't end with the resurrection; they start with it. For example, the presence of the Risen Christ among Luke and his people, freeing them, enlightening them, delivering them, loving them, healing them, accompanying them as they walked from the year 33 to the year 80 as a community of believers was what created Luke's version of the gospel and of the church. That marks a third and new stage of revelation.

Stages of Revelation

The initial stage of divine revelation occurred in creation. God communicated Godself to us in the universe and its workings. Through contemplating the stars and planets, mountains and seas, plants and trees, animals and birds, men and women — and all of these creatures in relationship — we recognize God's goodness, oneness, truth, beauty, wonder, fidelity, and love. Thus, God is available to *all* peoples, all religions, and all of history.

Second is the Jewish stage of revelation. This is where a group of people in Egypt called "the Hebrews" encountered God, who called them out of slavery into freedom and into a people. While they were enslaved in Egypt, the Hebrews were not genetically one people, but a number of groups of slaves, all apparently sharing Semitic Near Eastern origins. The most important thing they had in common was their enslavement. What drew them together into a people was a spiritual vision and a common struggle.

But they were not initially one race or one people. In fact, hardly anybody on this earth is. We all came from a series of barbarian tribes that kept mixing and intermarrying through the centuries. Some like to think they're part of a pure race. There's no such thing. We're all just "people." That's what the Book of Genesis is saying (see Gen. 11).

But humans love isolating their own group, calling it a special race, and claiming to be better than others. That's what the Jews did after God brought them together. This collection of "Hebrews," after they finally got their act together, seemed pretty special to themselves.

They felt their power as a people and they experienced God's presence. Soon they began to think God had revealed Godself to them and not to anybody else, although this is strongly repudiated by the universalist theme that develops in the prophets, especially Isaiah and Zechariah (see Isa. 2:2–4; 25:6–8; 55:1–11; 56:6–8; 60:11–14; Zech. 8:20–23). Nevertheless, the important point is they entered the second stage of revelation: they understood that God was making a personal self-disclosure to the whole human race.

Now the question is: How was God revealing God to them? The answer is: In events, in history, in relationships, and in what was happening around them. Action and reality were very important for the Jewish mind. What is the Jewish notion of truth? For the Jew, truth is, in fact, "what's happening." The Hebrew people lived before the modern age, without a scientific, objective knowledge of truth and falsity. For them, to be in the truth was not to tell lies. Truth was an action, not a concept. Truth had to do with telling what was really happening; falsity meant knowing what was really happening but telling lies or being deceitful about it.

Our modern "need" for scientific and historical truth is why most of us have so much trouble with the Bible. Today we are asking historical and scientific questions, establishing contemporary criteria of truth and fact on religious texts written thousands of years ago. Objective truth or fact was not a criterion to them at all. For them, truth was something personal, something shared, a social contract; if I shared something with you knowing in fact that it was not the case, then I was being untruthful.

In the early Hebrew mind, truth was not opposed to error because the Hebrews did not possess our abstract notion of truth and error. They were not Platonic, nor are most Jews to this day. In every century, however, Christianity has had to fight some form of Gnosticism. Much institutional theology, Catholic and Protestant, continues to reflect more a Platonic world of ideas and ideals than the Hebraic concreteness of Jesus.

Telling the truth and telling lies are actions, not abstract notions. Truth is the opposite of telling lies, not the opposite of error. That distinction might seem unimportant, but it kept the idea of truth very personal and down to earth, as opposed to the highly metaphysical and abstract notion of truth that many conservative Catholics have today.

In reflecting on the events of their history, the Jewish people came to recognize God's self-disclosure and self-communication. This experience grew and evolved. As generations passed, they increasingly understood how God was present to them. They expressed this development in their sacred writings.

Even though we say that the Bible is inspired in its entirety, among the biblical books there are varying degrees of God's self-communication. This variation is also found in different sentences, passages, paragraphs, and chapters of each scriptural book. All biblical passages are not all equally important nor equally revelatory of God. The Jewish people understood this. For example, you can read chapters and chapters in the Book of Numbers or Leviticus and say, "I don't know what this is telling me about God." It probably isn't telling you a whole lot except the patterns to avoid.

Furthermore, while some chapters aren't telling you much about God, other chapters may assert something we know now to be factually untrue, erroneous, mistaken, or unreal. "For our knowledge is imperfect, and our prophesying is imperfect.... We see indistinctly as in a mirror" (1 Cor. 13:9, 12). In the Bible, there are varying degrees of importance in God's self-revelation.

Because the Hebrew experience of God grew and evolved, the Hebrews increasingly understood who God was and how God relates to humans. In the beginning, to them, God was very legalistic and minimalistic. But their understanding continued to increase, reaching its heights in the Psalms, the Prophets, and the story of Job. The prophets understood the spiritual nature of the heart of God and how it liberates the human heart. But back in Genesis and Exodus, the Hebrew people were just at the beginning stages of that understanding, for example, in their apparent acceptance of killing, slavery, and polygamy. This is not to say those early books were unimportant; they simply marked the beginnings of divine revelation and the human faith response.

But already, the key revelation image is present — the Exodus story. There's where they started their faith journey and grew from it. The text begins its long travail with God and with itself.

The third stage of divine revelation was inaugurated by the Jesus experience. We believe that Jesus received fully in his own person what God was saying, but he also received it gradually.

How did he come to receive it? Just as you and I do, through walking the journey, through trial and error, through ups and downs, through living day one, day two and day three, and year twenty-one, twenty-two, twenty-three. God has given us this experience called life, which is intimately tied to time. Time is an essential ingredient in the human faith-adventure.

Why couldn't Jesus have appeared as a fully mature man seated on a golden pillow in the middle of Israel armed with the truths of all times and simply handed us the Constitution of Reality? He didn't. He walked a journey and learned what he knew, just as you and I do. As Jesus grew in wisdom, age, and grace, the revelation of the heart of God was growing in him also. Jesus in his life gives a faith response to the revelation of the Father. He manifests the two sides of the coin, revelation and faith. Jesus' faith did not falter. He learned what it meant to be a son through suffering (*passio*) (Heb. 5:7).

The verb "to suffer" means "to undergo." Related to our word "passive," it reflects the passive mode of living, which means to let reality impinge on you, to let things touch you and change you. In contrast, to impose yourself on reality is the active mode of living, which means you are defining who you are and what reality is. It is very telling that we speak of the "passion" of Christ as redemptive more than the "action!" The passive mode — the suffering mode — is where you are vulnerable, naked, and teachable, not manipulating things around you. In this passive mode, you are not forcing events, but letting your eyes be cleared and your heart be exposed more and more each day.

Today's word for the passive mode of living is "openness," a word we delight in. It indicates you are vulnerable to the people and events around you; you're open before the world and you allow it to speak to you. In this way, you let come into you all the revelation God wants to communicate. You don't deny it or dissect it; you let it come in and you respond to it in faith.

Let's say two people are listening to me talk. One person doesn't agree with 80 percent of what I say and walks away complaining and disappointed. The person of faith perceives the 20 percent of truth I spoke and gets all excited about it. After many years as a priest, I can say that it's delightful to be spiritual director of a person like the latter. The first person will come to see me and concentrate on the 80 percent of their life that's horrible or the 80 percent of what I said they didn't agree with. I guess there's a place for that. But then I see the people who are aware of the 80 percent that may be bad, and they're so delighted with the 20 percent that's good, they just keep kissing it, enjoying it, celebrating it, and sharing it. That's what I call a faith response! As you study Luke's Gospel along with my reflections on it, I encourage you to let reality come in and speak to you. Let everything speak to you.

Once upon a time a small Jewish boy went to his rabbi and said he didn't know how to love God. "How can I love God since I've never seen him?" explained the boy. "I think I understand how to love my mother, my father, my brother, my little sister, and even the people in our neighborhood, but I don't know how I'm supposed to love God."

The rabbi looked at the little boy and said, "Start with a stone. Try to love a stone. Try to be present to the most simple and basic thing in reality so you can see its goodness and beauty. Then let that goodness and beauty come into you. Let it speak to you. Start with a stone." The boy nodded with understanding.

"Then, when you can love a stone," the rabbi continued, "try a flower. See if you can love a flower. See if you can be present to it and let its beauty come into you. See if you can let its life come into you and you can give yourself to it. You don't have to pluck it, possess it, or destroy it. You can just love it over there in the garden." The boy nodded again.

"I'm not saying it's wrong to pick flowers," added the rabbi. "I'm asking you to learn something from the flower without putting it in a vase." The boy smiled, which meant he understood — or maybe he didn't. Just in case he didn't, the rabbi chose the boy's pet dog as the next object of loving and listening. The boy nodded and smiled when the rabbi talked about his dog; he even said, "Yes, Rabbi."

"Then," the rabbi went on, "try to love the sky and the mountains, the beauty of all creation. Try to be present to it in its many forms. Let it speak to you and let it come into you." The boy sensed the rabbi wanted to say some more, so he nodded again, as if he understood.

"Then," the rabbi said, "try to love a woman. Try to be faithful to a woman and sacrifice yourself for her. After you have loved a stone, a flower, your little dog, the mountain, the sky, and a woman, then you'll be ready to love God."

How lovely and how true! Too many people have tried to short-circuit the process of learning to love God. Instead of starting with a stone and working their way up to God, they quickly pretend to have some immediate contact with divine revelation. I don't want to discourage anyone from running to God, but some people don't yet know how to run or how to love the stones. They don't yet know how to perceive, how to be faithful, how to sacrifice, how to see — and not control. They probably try to control because, like the rest of us, they feel weak, alienated, and out of communion with reality. But control never works in the spiritual life. The "undergoing" (passion) teaches more than the fixing and explaining (action).

People with little or no patience for communing with stones, flowers, pets, or human beings will probably not have much more patience communing directly with God. Because they have not done their homework, they will most likely distort the revelation of God and use it for their own purposes. The false, egocentric self, disconnected from union, will be unable to see things correctly or enjoy them for themselves. The fragmented person seems to fragment everything else. The reconnected person sees rightly and, not surprisingly, sees God too.

Divine Revelation and Faith Community

If it is true that God's self-revelation was most fully received in the human consciousness of Jesus, then the question arises: Where is God's self-revelation being received today? This is a question Luke was dealing with too, as was Luke's community.

The early Christians could not conceive that divine revelation had ceased to happen, so their question is: How and where is it happening now? The answer Luke's community gave, if put in twentieth-century theological language, would go something like this: "If God's self-revelation was most fully received in the human consciousness of Jesus Christ, then the ongoing, living church — the faith community that calls itself the Body of Christ — must now be the primary place of God's revelation. The ongoing faith-revelation dialogue should be occurring between God and the living organism of the church. That's where God's voice should be most heard and most responded to, because we as a community of believers have the mind of Christ." The church in all its varied forms and holistic life was being called to put on the mind that was in Christ Jesus (Phil. 2:5).

To us in the twentieth century, excommunication refers to a legal or canonical status based on a decision made by the official church hierarchy or imposed by canon law. To the first-century Christians, excommunication was a state of the human heart; it came about through a series of choices that put an individual outside the loving faith community. In this sense, excommunication has always been far more widespread than we might think.

Through the centuries of the church, many people have lived very cut-off, excommunicated lives, lives disconnected from the faith community; such people often had their own personal copies of the Bible which they read and in which they "found salvation" in an ideological sense. Such private faith disconnected from the whole is not a gospel notion of salvation. For Luke, salvation can be understood only within the living Body of Christ in the living church. This is even more evident in his second book, the Acts of the Apostles.

Thus — and this is true for us today — the ongoing place of God's revelation is groups of people who have put on the mind of Christ, living together in various ways and loving one another. Those are the people who, as a community, listen to God. *The Bible was given to a community of believers, not to isolated individuals. In this sense, a solitary person cannot hear God's word except in the context of a loving community, because such a cut-off person will necessarily be a fear-filled person, a hurt person, or a negative person, and one whose vision will be myopic, small, and diminished.*

That's what Catholic theology has always meant when it said: The church interprets the Word of God. Unfortunately, "church" became identified with an institution and its management. There is a correct and authentic way to understand the expression "church" in the statement: "Only the church can interpret the Word of God." The authentic church is not simply made up of priests, bishops, and popes, but much more people who can listen, hear, and be taught (That is what "disciple" means). Those are the people who can fittingly receive and use the Word of God. Proof-texting by power seekers and isolated idealists has never borne any fruit for history. We are ready to do much better now.

It may sound to some that I'm standing on both sides of the fence, or even the wrong side. I'm giving this big pitch for the church, saying: "The church is everything. The community is where the presence of God is at. The Bible is about the church; it's a document of the church. It doesn't make any sense outside the church community; and when it's used without the church it's misused." On the other side, I'm saying:

"Religion isn't where it's at. Religion is a waste of time. God is not about creating religions on earth."

The confusion occurs because most people equate religion and church, and I'm saying they're not the same thing. When I use the word "church," I mean people gathered in faith and love with one another and with their Lord; church is an experience that is personal, shared, organic, and life-giving. When I use the word "religion," I refer to the collection of rituals, dogmas, and other means people have developed to help make them feel saved — whatever they mean by that term.

In this sense, religion often misses the good news we have been given through revelation in the Judeo-Christian tradition. The good news is that the salvation question is already answered. God loves us unconditionally. We are loved by God. Period. Our life should be a going forward from that question. The salvation question is taken care of: You don't have to work for salvation; you don't have to spin prayer wheels to get it; you don't need to perform any magical rituals to talk God into loving you. That question has been resolved forever, but the Christian church usually doesn't believe it. We still perform rituals to get God to love us and to convince ourselves that we are lovable.

Convincing ourselves is largely what we're doing in churches. And we *do* need convincing! The reason we use celebrations, rituals, sacramentals, and Scripture is because we do indeed need to convince ourselves every day, ten times a day, that God could love us. But we don't need to convince God to love us. That's a given.

The Bible as Gift to the Church

We must never forget that the church came first. The church produced the Bible; the Bible did not produce the church, although it does continue to sustain it, challenge it, and reform it. In the second and third centuries, the faith community decided which of the sacred books were to be included in what we now call the Bible. For Catholics, only at the Council of Trent in the sixteenth century did the church unequivocally list those Scriptures included in the biblical canon as "inspired."

For centuries, the early Christians used a wide variety of holy books, letters, and texts. Some early communities stressed certain sacred texts more than others. Gradually a biblical tradition developed. For readings in the faith assembly, they narrowed down the gospel writings to four books. Additionally available at the time were the Gospel of Barnabas, the Gospel of Thomas, and a number of other gospel writings not read universally. It is as though the church said of these other writings: "We're not saying these aren't faith expressions, but they do not express the holistic vision of Jesus this church holds as a unified faith community." So they eliminated from the Bible all but the four gospels we use today: Matthew, Mark, Luke, and John.

But the important point is that the church — the believing community — was making all these decisions. The living tradition decided which documents best mirrored its communal truth.

One problem in theological seminaries during the twentieth century has been a lack of historical perspective. I was lucky to have studied theology after Vatican II. Before then, in great part, when a seminarian came into first-year theology, five theological volumes were waiting on his desk. During the next four years, his task was to master the contents of those five books. They were full of conclusions. A seminarian's task in theology was to study, memorize, and defend those conclusions.

What changed in seminaries after Vatican II was that we stopped studying just the conclusions. We also studied the process. We faced the question: "How did the church arrive at those conclusions in the first place?" In class we'd review those conclusions, century by century. For example, we'd take the theme of "grace" and begin by studying the Hebrew Scriptures and their understanding of "election." In Deuteronomy and the Prophets, we saw how God's love came to the chosen people freely and unearned. God's message to them was: "I didn't choose you because you were the best people, I simply chose you because I chose you." That's the beginning of the theme of grace.

Then we studied the Christian Scriptures to understand grace in the life of Jesus; we sought to know how Jesus spoke about grace. Then we studied the Pauline letters to understand grace in the life of Paul; in his writings we found a development that didn't seem to be in the gospels. Theologically, there's almost always a development from Jesus to Paul, which shows that the early church understood two things: first, that there is a development of doctrine in the church and, second, that divine revelation was still going on after Jesus died, though Paul taught that it had to begin with Jesus' words.

A clear example of doctrinal development is what Paul did with Jesus' teaching on marriage. Given the available data that we have about Jesus' teaching, his position was hard and fast against divorce under any circumstances. But, twenty-five years later, we observe Paul making exceptions (see 1 Cor. 7:12–16). Yet we call Paul's writings the inspired word of God just as much as we call the Gospels of Matthew, Mark, Luke, and John.

It's obvious Jesus and Paul were often saying different things. It's amazing to me that, even with historical study, many people don't see the obvious development of morals and doctrine in the Scriptures; and yet all the books are "inspired."

Continuing with the issue of grace after Paul, we studied what the first church councils said on the topic; we studied what a certain saint contributed to the picture as well as the special emphasis given by St. Augustine. We studied theological thinking on the topic of grace in the High Middle Ages, the Scholastic period, the Council of Trent, and then Vatican II. The delightful thing was that with a historical perspective you could mark the doctrinal development of grace on a time graph. Century by century, the graph would indicate changes the church was making in its understanding of grace: Now they were emphasizing this theme; now they were going in this new direction; now grace was seen as more Pelagian and "earned"; now it was seen more given by God and "unearned." It was exciting to chart through the centuries the progress and process of various theological themes.

Vatican II brought us right back to the heart of things in terms of a biblical theology. It told us to study *salvation history,* not just the conclusions. That's the grace of the age that you and I live in, that our church has returned, almost overnight, to a biblical theology with a historical perspective.

This return proved cataclysmic for our faith communities, however, because priests and people had never been trained in a biblical way of thinking. How many Bible quotes did Catholics know? Only a few, those that justified our papacy, our Mass, and our sacramental system: "Thou art Peter and upon this rock I will build my church" or "Whose sins ye shall forgive, they are forgiven them" or "This is my body, this is my blood" or "Go and baptize all nations."

Because we were not seriously studying the Scriptures, we didn't even know what a biblical theology was. Most Bible teachers around at the time of Vatican II were Catholic fundamentalists and literalists. Most did not teach the historical process, but taught prefabricated conclusions and used sacred quotations as "proof."

The Catholic who needed quick authoritative answers became dogmatic or legalistic. The Protestant who needed quick authoritative answers became a fundamentalist. But they were both the same personality type, the same temperament. Both sought surety, superiority, and control instead of struggling with the mysteries that must be struggled with.

Once people began to follow the Vatican II direction, they found themselves back in the mainline tradition of Christian biblical theology. Here, the challenge was to gather together the reflections of believers over the past two thousand years.

The biblical tradition is what I want to explore in these chapters, so I'm going to be working with that process: as we read how Jesus was living the process, as we infer how the Lucan community was living the process, and as we watch how we at the end of the twentieth century are living the process — struggling with the mysteries of life, death, freedom, and grace.

Jesus' struggle with these mysteries is the meaning of the incarnation. We will walk with Jesus because that's what Luke has done. Luke also lived his life among a faith community in the spirit of Jesus, and we will follow his process too. At the same time, we'll be reflecting on our own faith process in light of Jesus' process and that of the Lucan community. I promise not to use the Bible apart from the context of a living faith community that acts and interacts, challenges and supports.

The Whole-Church Perspective

Jesus Christ is our truth. That truth was and continues to be communicated to the church in its entirety for the benefit of the church in its entirety. That whole-church perspective should provide a good antidote for any pride and conceit any of us might have, since none of us in our finite minds and experience can begin to comprehend the whole Christ or even the whole church. Each of us is one little piece of the grand Christ mosaic, and we rejoice in that and give ourselves to it. But it is important to remain conscious that we are only one little part of the whole. As long as we stay in that consciousness, we will continue to remain available to the truth as it comes to us.

Just as Jesus Christ is the truth and the divine Word, so the whole church in its varied forms as the ongoing Body of Christ is the ongoing Word and the ongoing context for interpreting the word. Only the church in its shared life can understand the faith writings of a Luke or a John, whatever those writings might be.

I have stated this point before, but it bears repeating: It has been misleading in many cases simply to call the Bible the "Word of God," because what some people mean by "Word of God" is a divine word-for-word dictation, which is misleading; and what other people mean that every word in Scripture has equal authoritative value, which is also misleading; still others mean by "Word of God" that the scriptural words are timeless and free from cultural conditioning, which is also misleading, since no words expressed in human language can be free from the constraints of history and culture.

I'm all for saying that the Bible is the Word of God, but if you don't have to struggle to know what that phrase means, and you say it quickly and glibly, you may easily slip into any or all of those three common misunderstandings.

What is the inspired level of the Bible, then? *It is to understand what the author was actually asserting, what the author was really trying to say when he or she wrote the text.* That's what's inspired and objective. It takes prayer and study to attempt an understanding of that. Faith and community will show us how to transfer the inspired message to our parallel situations.

In addition to the meaning Luke is trying to convey, his words have a cultural conditioning. They are not timeless words; they are words that meant something in Luke's day. Because certain words and expressions change their meaning over time, we have to make new biblical translations. Thus, I think people do themselves a great disservice when they insist on using only the King James Version of the Bible, because instead of leading you deeper into the Word of God the words in that translation whose meanings have changed may move you farther away from the Word. Good translators change outdated idioms into ways we say the same things today. Scriptural translating, which must also be done in the context of a faith community, takes genius and the gift of wisdom: to learn how to say to us what Luke was trying to say to his community. It's the Spirit's gift to the ministry of teaching in the church that helps make that transfer.

When you read the Bible, it is being filtered through your experience, your level of maturity, your level of faith development, your intellectual capacity, your prejudices and preferences. Therefore, *everyone who reads the Bible interprets it; that's the only way it can*

be. God understands that. The meaning has to come filtered through your mind and experience. It's not bad that we all necessarily interpret the Bible. But if you take your interpretation of a certain passage and absolutize it, saying, "Everybody's got to understand this passage the same way I do," that's when you're taking on an authority that only the church in its total life can take.

The Catholic Church, by the way, has made authoritative interpretations about very few passages. The church has hardly ever said about a particular passage: "This is the authoritative way to interpret this passage and it may be understood in no other way." Catholics enjoy much leeway in interpreting the scriptural text.

Ironically, it is a common Protestant misunderstanding that Catholics are so under the law that the pope sends out edicts from time to time to tell us exactly how to interpret each line of the sacred text. As a matter of fact, the Catholic failing is rather on the other end; we've received hardly any direction from our leadership. People who think the Catholic Church is monolithically controlling the thoughts of its people in scriptural matters are far from the truth. We get very little direction from on high in understanding the Bible, in learning how to interpret it, and in using it. Our problem is more that we are authoritarian about presumed tradition.

As we reflect on the Lucan text, I presume you have at your side a technical biblical commentary on Luke. I will offer selected comments about different topics in Luke. I hope you will find them interesting, helpful, and life-giving for your faith and understanding of the good news. I will respond to Luke's text, more or less line by line, paragraph by paragraph, gathering the spirit and understanding there, but I preface this with a quick overview of some major Lucan themes.

Luke and His Gospel

Luke is a gentile, that is, a non-Jew. From his writings it is obvious his concerns are different from the Jewish Matthew. Luke is perhaps a Roman or a Syrian and certainly a convert.

He is also well-educated, indicated by the classic and polished writing style of his text. He was educated in the Greek tradition, so he does not think like a Jewish theologian. Because he was brought up in a "pagan" culture, his familiar concepts, inbred ideas, and Greek ways of thinking are very non-Jewish. Although he reverences Jerusalem and its temple as the place which gave us Jesus, Luke is not at home there, either geographically or culturally. In fact, he probably never visited Jerusalem.

As we find out in the Acts of the Apostles, it seems likely that Luke met Paul on his second missionary journey and traveled with him for some time. So Luke perhaps enjoyed a friendship and ministering relationship with Paul, and was probably influenced by his thought. It has traditionally been believed that Luke also knew about Mary the mother of Jesus. Luke, more than any of the other evangelists, writes about Mary. Most of what we know about her comes from Luke. Luke is a second generation Christian. The first generation knew Jesus face to face. The second-generation never saw the historical Jesus.

It is obvious that Luke has read and is familiar with Mark's Gospel, probably written between the years 65 and 70. This primary gospel, available to Luke, had been passed around for about twenty years, so everybody knew it. Luke counts on that familiarity, because he adapts almost one-third of his text from Mark. The first source of Luke's Gospel is a text biblical scholars deduce must have existed, which they call the Q Document.

The Gospels of Mark, Matthew, and Luke are often referred to as the synoptic gospels. "Synoptic" means, literally, "with the same eyes," or "from the same perspective." Luke does present a lot of the same stories and themes found in Mark and Matthew, but he will give them a slightly different emphasis. Luke used almost 60 percent of Mark's Gospel to create his own text, but often he'll change Mark's words here or there. It is the study of those word changes, along with the themes he develops, that has allowed Scripture scholars to clarify the points Luke wants to make, to discern his biases, and to identify the particular concerns of his Christian community.

During the 60s, when Mark was writing and the supposed Q Document was making the rounds, Christians were not so sure where Judaism left off and Christianity began. But by the year 80 it was becoming very clear, theologically, politically, and culturally, that these two were different religions.

Although we know and can infer a lot about Luke's thinking, we really don't know where he lived and wrote. Scholars are not sure where Luke's community was located; some think Syria. The consensus is Luke was part of a faith community somewhere in Asia Minor. Around the year 80, Christians were struggling with a new set of questions about Jesus. In his gospel, Luke was trying to answer those questions.

Characteristics of Luke's Gospel

MISSIONARY. The sense we get from studying the gospel text is that Luke's community is like a missionary center. People there are concerned about evangelism and are probably sending missionaries out in teams, at least to nearby communities. This would be no surprise, especially if Luke himself had been a missionary with Paul.

UNIVERSAL. Luke wanted his missionary teams equipped to communicate a Jesus Christ who is universal, whose message is a worldwide one, directed not only to Jews but to peoples of all races and religions. Called the Universal Gospel, Luke is the most catholic of the evangelists. He doesn't want to eliminate anyone from the purview of Christ. He communicates a Jesus who is life-giving and unifying for all peoples of the earth.

In contrast, although Matthew is trying to break away from Judaism, he is afraid to be totally universalist because that would really upset the conservatives in his community. So he merely nudges the universal theme a few steps, but Luke really develops it.

That Luke was a disciple of Paul makes sense here because Paul was the apostle to the gentiles; his concern was to go beyond Judaism. By Luke's day, they've made the break; they see themselves almost as a new religion, though still rooted in Judaism. This perspective is clearly reflected in Luke. He has the big picture.

Since he is most likely not a Jew himself, he doesn't come to Jesus' message with all the Jewish biases. He doesn't fear displeasing the Jewish contingent of Christians. Luke behaves and thinks much like a convert to Catholicism who didn't grow up with some of the biases born-Catholics have.

For example, I was talking to a priest in California who joined the church after Vatican II. He was presiding at Mass one day and the lector announced, "Today is First Friday." He wondered, "Why is he telling them it's the first Friday?" The next day the same lector announced it was First Saturday. So in the sacristy afterward he asked the lector, "Why do you tell the people it's the first Friday and Saturday?" The puzzled lector said, "Don't you know?" That's a small example of what born-Catholics grow up with that most converts know nothing about.

Like a convert, Luke doesn't seem to be bothered or anxious about all those Jewish customs. In fact, he may never have been to Israel, because his Holy Land geography is sometimes confused, and you can tell he really doesn't know where certain cities are.

FORGIVENESS. Luke's Gospel is the most broad-minded and the most forgiving. Every chance he gets, Luke has Jesus forgiving people, right up to the good thief on the cross. Luke presents Jesus as a totally forgiving person, because he wants to broaden the notion of Jesus and the faith communities who follow his Way. Already in these first decades of the church, many have begun to depict Jesus as a narrowing, provincial kind of Messiah available only to Jews who want to convert, and Luke wants to counteract that.

MERCY AND UNIVERSAL SALVATION. Luke is quite ready to see God as generous, gratuitous, and merciful, all the way to the cross. Mercy and inclusivity are emphasized a great deal in Luke, much more so than in Matthew or Mark. He emphasizes Jesus' ministry to social outcasts, to gentiles, to the poor. Everyone is being called to salvation in Christ; there seems to be no limit to God's mercy and forgiveness. Even though it will be most difficult for the rich to enter the kingdom of heaven, Luke has Jesus assure them that nothing is impossible with God.

WOMEN. In this broad-minded approach, Luke's sacred text is also called the gospel of women. Far more than any other evangelist, Luke brings women into Jesus' life and shows Jesus' unique way of relating to women. Luke always portrays women in a good light. He wants to make Jesus available to the forgotten and diminished half of the human race. In that era, women were looked down upon, they were not considered educated, and their opinion carried little weight. In contrast, Luke portrays women as competent, sensible, valuable — and personally valued by Jesus.

THE "LONG HAUL." By Luke's day, the church's perspective was changing from the "short run" to the "long haul." During the years from 50 to 80, Christian thinkers were constantly churning out new theology in an attempt to understand their present experience. Since Jesus had not returned in glory as expected, they realized the "short-run" theological approach was no longer viable. When Luke comes along, he's heading for the "long haul" and knows it.

HOLY SPIRIT. In a very real sense, as the church was able to admit that the Messiah's Second Coming was no longer imminent, a new religion called Christianity began forming. The key question they needed to deal with was: What is this Jesus all about? To begin to answer that question Luke's Gospel focused on the Holy Spirit. More than in any other gospel, the Holy Spirit is constantly spoken of; and that leads him into writing the Acts of the Apostles, often called the gospel of the Holy Spirit.

We find, therefore, in Luke a well-developed theology of the Holy Spirit. First of all, Luke frequently mentions the Holy Spirit; he also invokes the necessity of the Holy Spirit, and announces that they are now living in the reign of the Spirit. His emphasis is not so much that Jesus will return again, but that Jesus has sent his Spirit, and those of us who call upon that Spirit and rely upon it are going to be prepared to live in the "New Age." Note that this expression is first "ours" and we should not be afraid of it. Jesus himself uses it in Matthew 19:26.

Neither Mark nor Matthew taught much about the Holy Spirit. In contrast, Luke is preoccupied and filled with a sense of the Holy Spirit. For Luke, the Spirit is behind everything. If you were to ask Luke: "If Jesus isn't going to return, how is Jesus here among us?" He would answer: "Jesus is present among us in his Holy Spirit."

THE KINGDOM NOW. For Luke, the Parousia, the Second Coming, is already a present reality. In the early days of the church, they had been expecting Christ to come on clouds of glory to inaugurate the kingdom. Luke says, in effect, "The kingdom is right now. The Christ has come. The presence of Jesus is among us. Let us rejoice in it, let us live in it. And don't worry about the 'final days.'" In other words, the presence of the Christ is alive among us now. To Luke, the date the historical risen Jesus is scheduled to return is an academic question. It doesn't matter at all.

Very often in Luke's Gospel you will observe the words "now" and "today." "Now is the time...." "Today has salvation come to your house." Luke's Gospel is filled with a sense of God's immanence and the necessity for us to be aware and see. Everything you need is available to you, Luke assures us. In that sense, he is very true to Jesus, who described the kingdom as here and now, not as a future kingdom. Much of church history has been preoccupied with the kingdom to come; for Luke, Jesus was preoccupied with the kingdom now.*

That seems to be where our contemporary church is right now, and that's why we have all this talk of "end-times" and "rapture." Such talk is used to avoid what Jesus primarily preached, "the kingdom now," and what Luke primarily preached, "Today is the day of salvation; live it now because now is what you have, for sure." Luke does not ever deny the Second Coming or eternal life; but he stresses a "present eschatology," as the theologians say, rather than a "future eschatology."

A BIAS TOWARD THE BOTTOM. Luke's has also been called the gospel of absolute renunciation. For Luke, to be a disciple one has to let go of everything — not just money or other external idols but inner idols and ego concerns, too. Luke advocates, more than any of the other gospels, radically new social patterns of relationship. His is an upside-down gospel. Scripture scholars call it the theme of reversal. *"The first will be last and the last will be first"* (13:30). Luke uses every story he can to show that what impresses people does not impress God, and that people who think they are at the top are often, in God's eyes, at the bottom, and people who think they are at the bottom are, in God's eyes, often at the top. It's an attempt to subvert our human admiration of power, ambition, and glory. Luke is often called the gospel of the poor.

NEW SOCIAL RELATIONSHIPS. Luke presents Jesus advocating a new social pattern, a much more horizontal pattern than the hierarchy of exploitation and domination of his day — and ours. I think it is fair to say that Jesus was a threat to the social-political system of his day in the same way that Gandhi was a threat to the British empire. Neither

---

*Our preoccupation with the future kingdom is not surprising. Apocalyptic turning to the future happens in any age when people are facing many difficult problems. Today's economic pressures seem insurmountable; social problems have grown so gargantuan we don't know how to deal with them. Apocalyptic thinking is quite understandable. In ages like ours, the natural theology that arises is future-focused. We can't deal with the present because its problems are too overwhelming, so we focus on envisioning a more hopeful future. The kingdom obviously isn't here now, we say, but our faith assures us that it will soon come.

Jesus nor Gandhi was *outrightly* teaching political change. But they were teaching people new attitudes about who they are and how they have to work together. Of course, when you do that, you're talking about social revolution, no matter what you may want to call it.*

NONVIOLENCE. Jesus was, however, not ever directly concerned with any kind of anti-Roman overthrow. At that time, the Jews were an oppressed people; the Romans were controlling their country. Jesus never seemed to teach overthrow, or even encourage it. However, it is interesting that one of his apostles was Simon the Zealot. Today, we'd call him Simon the Radical. In Jesus' day, Zealots were the group questioning the system; they even planned to overthrow the system by means of violence. Why, in Luke's mind did Jesus choose such a person as his apostle? To convert him to nonviolence? That's partially believable, from the many nonviolence passages we find in Luke.

Jesus' death itself is the most dramatic teaching of a way to attack evil other than the way of violence: by taking it into himself and triumphing over it by love, Jesus reveals the lie of scapegoating. Gandhi said that every major religion on this earth realizes that Jesus was teaching nonviolence and died a dramatic nonviolent death, except one: Christianity! Christianity has never been able to see its leader's commitment to nonviolence. It's too demanding; it's too close to home for us to see and admit this. Any intelligent outsider will say, "Oh, yes,

---

*That's exactly what's happening in many countries today. As people start to think differently about who they are, they become empowered, conscienticized, as we say. Their level of consciousness is raised; their sense of their own personhood is heightened. We Americans went through that two hundred years ago, in the founding of our nation. It's a shame that we lack sympathy for people doing the same thing today. All people have to be allowed the freedom to discover who they really are as persons and as community.

But know that when you are the agent of change, freeing people in that sense, you are always going to be a threat to the powers that be. The powerful often have a vested interest in keeping people dumb, women unconscious, and groups disunited. Many are old enough to remember the formation of labor unions in this country. During the first part of this century, people started becoming aware of their power, individually and together. As soon as they did that, they became a threat to the powers that be. This is the easiest way to understand why the state would conspire in the crucifixion of Jesus. What did Rome have to gain from it? We can see how he was questioning Israel and the established religion. But why was he crucified? Remember that crucifixion was not a Jewish form of execution; it was a Roman political form of execution. If Jesus' teaching was a threat to the current social-political system, then he would be seen as worthy of death. Otherwise Rome would have had no interest in a mere religious upstart.

obviously nonviolence is what he's teaching." But Christianity seems unable to see or teach what Jesus taught, because it would demand that we become nonviolent too. Luke seems to have already accepted this teaching as normative.

DANGER OF POWER. In this new social pattern of relationships, there is no room for people to oppress others. There is no room for a pattern that says some have all the power and others are always on the bottom. For Luke, the Christian community is clearly a co-operative system, a system not of domination, but of servanthood, of sharing, honoring women, caring for the poor, giving away surplus possessions. With no place for aspirations to be rich or violent, it teaches service and humility instead of power and domination. It's an upside-down ethic that Jesus teaches and Luke emphasizes.

THE ABSOLUTENESS OF GOD'S REIGN. Although Jesus never attacks Herod or Pilate, he never defers to them either. It's an interesting middle position. In Luke's Gospel, he calls Herod "that fox." "Foxy" has a warm feeling in our language, but I'm told by Scripture scholars that it doesn't have that connotation at all in Hebrew. To call someone a fox is to recognize that the person is devious. In Jesus' confrontation with Herod, he doesn't answer a single question (22:9). Jesus never defers to Pilot either. In several verbal exchanges with one who thinks he reigns, Jesus reasserts the absoluteness of God's reign. He speaks truth to the powerful without fear.

Recall the famous teaching when they bring Jesus the coin of tribute and he asks, *"Whose image is on it?"* They answer, *"Caesar's image is on it."* And he answers, *"Give to Caesar what is Caesar's and to God what is God's"* (20:24–25). Every Jew would know what this was saying, because they all knew the Book of Genesis: We were created in the image of God. The Greek word for "image" is *icon.* It's the very same word in both passages. "What do you give to God?" Jesus' answer is, "Whatever has God's icon stamped on it — which is everything created." Give him these coins if he wants them, but God's image is on everything else.

Luke's Missionary Focus

Again, it is important to remember that Luke writes and teaches from within a faith community. Why is that important? Because Luke's community is creating missionaries to go out and spread a new vision, and both those going out and those who send them out must ask themselves a very basic question: How can this Christian message be adapted to new cultures without compromising it?

The same question is posed to missionary societies today. I imagine the Maryknoll Fathers get together and ask themselves: How can we communicate the gospel in Africa? How can we communicate it in South America? How can we communicate it in Asia — and still be true to what Jesus is saying?

Luke helps deal with such questions because he wants to find a universal gospel. While the Maryknollers today are asking questions like: "Can we use the native language? Can we build churches in the architectural style we're used to? Can we adjust the liturgy to these different people?"

Realize Luke pondered questions like that when he set out to write his gospel, and he's looking for answers. It's important to know this because it helps explain why he writes the way he does. The question of persecution, for example, was very pressing in Luke's day: How can we continue to preach the good news since in some areas the government has imprisoned our missionaries? The most common persecution, today or in Luke's day, is not that people are being put in prison, stoned to death, or eaten by lions. Persecution more often takes the form of social and economic pressure.

In Luke's day, Christians were probably not able to get good jobs because of their faith. We tend to picture life back then very idealistically, imagining people walking around in a very simple society. That's a misconception. Then as always, people were playing games of exclusion, so those who happened to be "different" were victimized. A culture will always find a legitimate way to persecute outsiders.

Luke was dealing with a persecuted church. His people were experiencing rejection in a variety of forms, both in the missions and at home. That's why the issue of forgiveness was so important and constant. His people had to be free to forgive and let go of past hurts, or they wouldn't be able to be a church. There were a lot of hurting people around in Luke's era, and he had to give them a rationale for such suffering.

When Luke's Christians went out on missions, most likely they met people of very different backgrounds, people who were truly different from the Jewish folk they knew, who were familiar with the Scriptures and the law. Missionaries had to struggle with the question: Does Jesus want us to demand anything special of these different people? Does he love them as much as he loves us?

Just a few weeks ago, I was talking to a seasoned African missionary. He said, "When I first arrived in my mission territory, the people there had never practiced monogamous marriage. That first day the question I faced was: Do I walk into this tribe and tell them that every man has to let go of his extra wives if he wants to accept Jesus? Of course not. As a good missionary, I had to learn how to move the community toward that point slowly. It would have to be a process. My focus was on process."

Analogously, Luke's missionaries would have to help their listeners understand the mercy of God and gradually to recognize the gospel's implications. Luke didn't write his text isolated from the problems of life, the problems of faith, and the problems of society. It is precisely in light of those problems that Luke presents his gospel message.

This African missionary was telling me, for example, that he began to celebrate the Eucharist in a simple manner after giving a very basic evangelization, telling the people that God is Father, God is Love, and God is Goodness. He said to the people, "Now I'm going to celebrate a very simple meal of God's love with you. Those of you who join in this meal are entering into God's love." Then he held out the bread to them and said, "Whoever eats this bread believes that your people are one people. Do you know the implication of that? That means you can't hate one another anymore."

What he didn't know, however, was that in this particular tribe, it was the custom that men always ate together, while women and children ate separately. In their tribe, it was humiliating for a man to eat with a woman. Unwittingly, the priest had gathered men and women around the altar table and fed the bread to the men and women there. Naturally, this blew their minds, and the natives reacted strongly. The priest raised his voice over their murmurings and said, "In Christ, there is no distinction between male and female."

The people boggled at that statement. They wanted to know: "Who is this Christ anyway who makes no distinction between men and women?"

The priest tried to explain: "He is father to all. That means you are all brothers and sisters, and when you eat this bread you are all one in Christ." At this, some began to move away, because it was humiliating for men to eat with women. Culturally, they could not even allow themselves to share bread together.

The challenge was to find a way to communicate the gospel in this cultural context. For him, the Eucharist was the essence of the gospel, so his approach was simply to celebrate the Eucharist and explain as clearly as he could what it meant and what it implied. He did this day after day, year after year. In fifteen years, Christianity had created a social revolution in that tribe.

One day, the priest recalled, the men came and literally put their weapons at his feet, saying to him: "If the gospel you preach to us is true; if this Jesus, this Son of the Father, loves us in this total way; and if he is the Father of all of the people in our village and the Father of the people in the village down the road, then we can't kill them anymore." In fifteen years, this tribe learned what Western civilization has not learned in two thousand years, because here the gospel was preached in its purity and simplicity. The missionary had simply told them what God was saying and doing in the gospel.

In Western civilization we have sadly learned what can happen when people take that simple gospel Luke is preaching and distort it into religious denominations. The missionary said, "I figured there was no point in confusing these people by telling them about Lutherans, Presbyterians, Catholics, and Episcopalians. If Jesus wanted to come to these people, I just wanted to communicate the kingdom and the Father to them. After fifteen years, I had ten thousand practicing Christians who were celebrating the Eucharist.

"Then, a bishop from Rome, assigned to investigate the situation, asked me, 'Do these people know that they are Catholics?' and I said, 'No. I haven't told them that yet.'

"To which the startled bishop replied, 'You haven't told them that yet?' Then he pulled his head back and decided this situation was entirely out of control."

"But we have ten thousand Christians here," I repeated.

"But they have got to know they are Catholic," he insisted.

"They are a catholic people," the priest explained. "They are a universal people, open to all that God is saying and doing."

The bishop threw up his hands and returned to Rome.

After much thought, the missionary wondered if the bishop might not be right. Maybe he should at least teach the villagers about the seven sacraments. "We were," he said, "in effect, celebrating them in

very different ways, but celebrating them nevertheless. But I figured I'd
better make the people 'Catholic' and teach them that there are seven
sacraments. So I gathered some of the elders together and explained
that a sacrament is an encounter between God and humans; it is the
moment when we encounter God. And I told them there were seven
of these moments.

"They all looked puzzled, and finally one of them spoke up: 'But
we thought there were at least seven hundred!' It was at that moment
that I realized I would be limiting their perception of reality to insist
there were only seven moments when God encounters humans. These
people were already sacramentally minded and more incarnational
than we Westerners are. They had no trouble believing in sacramentalism — that God communicates with us in signs, symbols, rituals,
and gestures. Since their entire life was filled with rituals, gestures,
signs, and symbols, they couldn't imagine limiting these to seven."
Now that's a holistic, universal gospel.

Unfortunately, in Western civilization, we no longer have many of
the wise, courageous missionaries who preach that kind of gospel. My
point is the approach the missionary used with the village people in
Africa is the kind of gospel Luke was trying to preach and the kind
of Jesus he was trying to present, the Jesus to whom all the nations
could be open.

Another problem Luke was dealing with were the rich Christians.
At their eucharistic gatherings, Luke hears them saying, "We are all
one, we are all one." At the same time, Luke sees them not sharing
their wealth with the needy. Some who sit at the Lord's Table are living a lifestyle radically different from that of the less fortunate. The
dissonance in their community is becoming quite apparent, and Luke
seems very concerned about it. This concern is interesting, because
Luke himself, as well as being well educated, was probably a rich man,
or perhaps came from a wealthy family in Rome. Tradition always
had it that Luke was a physician.

Luke so struggles with the problem of rich Christians that one-
seventh of the teaching he puts in Jesus' mouth is a condemnation
of riches. Luke is the strongest of the evangelists on that point; in this
sense, his is the gospel of the poor. Luke simply cannot understand
wealthy people who live right next to poor people and do nothing for
them. To him, that is inconceivable. So the Gospel according to Luke
delivers very hard words to the rich.

Again, Luke's message is appropriate for today's American church, and for wherever people still do not see the impropriety and impossibility of preaching the gospel to a world which does not live out its implications. That's exactly what we have done: we've continued to read sacred texts but really don't expect them to change our lifestyle in any concrete way.

In many parts of the world, it is almost impossible to preach the gospel. A few weeks ago I was preaching in the islands of the West Indies. On island after island, I could see how the gospel had been watered down and dissolved into a cultural puddle. (The same thing is true generally in the United States.) The implications of the gospel go unmentioned here, so much so that, on some of the islands, I spent 80 percent of my time trying to undo the past. I couldn't proclaim the goodness of the Lord because they were holding on to, promoting, and perpetuating what I might call, in polite terms, "the past mistakes of the church," such as slavery, riches of the clergy, and many other practices which reflect lives not in tune with the gospel.

That blatant contradiction between message and action is holding us back in every part of the world. We preach a self-absorbed gospel of piety and religiosity, not a lifestyle gospel. Luke is preaching a lifestyle gospel, not a Sunday-churchy thing at all.

Luke is talking about living the gospel seven days a week. His gospel is so radical that if you truly believed its message it would call into question all the assumptions you currently hold about the way you live, how you use time, whom you relate to, how you marry, how much money you have. Everything you think and do would be called into question and viewed in a new way, because Jesus is Lord and Jesus is Love.

In his gospel Luke is also dealing with the problem of less-than-exemplary church leaders. We also have that problem in our contemporary church, not just in the West Indies. It has been a continual problem throughout the history of the church.

When I read the lives of the saints, I discovered many of them were working for the reform of the clergy. Although they began by preaching the gospel to the people in the towns and villages, they soon realized: "We're not going to get anywhere and we can't accomplish anything until we get the clergy converted and turned to the Lord."

During the first years of my own ministry, I was talking to teen-agers. Now I work more and more with priests, religious, and bishops.

Until we clergy get our act together, turn back to the Lord, start living a simple lifestyle and sharing life together, we simply don't have the right to preach the gospel. Many clergy today are powerless to preach the good news because they are not living a Christian lifestyle, which is what gives the greatest power to speak to people. The call to conversion applies not only to clergy, but to all of us. None of us has the right to speak the gospel message or the power to proclaim it until we begin living a new kind of life in tune with the gospel.

Luke is concerned about that contradiction between word and action, and he has apparently watched church leaders become very demanding and power-hungry. So in his gospel Luke redefines "authority." What does church authority mean to Luke? It means to serve God's people. To say the least, such upside-downness has been slow to catch on. Go to Europe and visit the lovely "pleasure palaces" of the bishop-princes. They are quite common.

The Gospel of Luke was written after the destruction of Jerusalem, which happened in the year 70. For the Jews, Jerusalem and the temple were the epitome of their religious symbolism, and its core had been utterly destroyed. For a Catholic, it would be as if Rome and the Vatican were bombed leaving nothing but rubble. There would be no center of our church to look at anymore. Catholics might wonder: "How can the church go on? Who is going to give the orders? Who's going to appoint the bishops? Whatever is going to happen to us?"

The destruction of Jerusalem was just as devastating for the Jewish people, and they had many of these same questions. Luke is writing shortly after the destruction of Jerusalem, so keep that fact in the back of your mind and it will help you understand certain events and teachings when we get to them.

Prayer is probably spoken of more in Luke's Gospel than anywhere else in the Christian Scriptures. It's as if he is saying to his community, "Many of our old friends were martyred, we've seen a lot of suffering, we've been through a lot together. The only way we've learned to survive is by prayer." This theme again reflects Luke's perspective of the "long haul."

He's not just talking about an activist Christianity, but also about a contemplative Christianity. He encourages us to be not only action-oriented but deep and centered as well. Because he constantly alludes to prayer, his is called the gospel of prayer. Before every major decision of Jesus and the apostles, there is a resting in prayer, a time of listening to God. Whenever Luke can find Jesus praying, he always mentions it, whereas the other gospels don't. We can assume Jesus did pray at these times, and Luke is the one who remembered to mention it. He recalls Jesus' frequent praying because it is a need now in his community — to remind people that Jesus prayed before he made major decisions.

You may wonder why Luke mentions Jesus' prayer and the others don't. It's not as if the evangelists are making up things about Jesus or lying; they are rather recalling those details of Jesus' life they think might be needed for the group they're addressing. I do the same thing myself. When I'm standing in front of a different group, I recall different information and stories. I preach according to the needs of the group I'm addressing. That's what each of the evangelists is doing: retelling the gospel for their specific audience. Scholars call this kind of analysis of the biblical text "form criticism." It's a common way Scripture has been studied in the last twenty years.

All in all, Luke is a good pastor, creatively adapting his message to the needs of his own people, trying especially to deal with the faith questions they ask.

Story Theology

Earlier civilizations used stories almost exclusively to teach their children, communicate with each other, and pass on their culture and values. A recent development in theology, called *story theology*, focuses on communicating the life, power, and revelation of God through stories. Though some claim that this is a new kind of theology, it is actually Jesus' favorite form of theology. In his parables, Jesus communicates his experience of God primarily through stories. Luke and the other evangelists use story theology too. Luke is telling the Jesus story as it shaped him. Therefore, the Gospel according to Luke is also a story about Luke.

What's the special power of a story? It gives you the ability to step into an event, move around in it, and make it your own. It's not something you put into a mental file folder like abstract objective teaching. It's a system of images and symbols which you can touch, hold, and play with. Therefore a story can be both healing and liberating. It doesn't set limits on reality nearly as much as abstract conceptual thought does.

We are rediscovering that people always communicate their deepest values by telling stories, and I find it exciting to discover this same pattern in Scripture. Have any of you in religious education sometimes felt badly about yourself, saying, "I wish I knew abstract theology and could read Raymond Brown or George Montague, but all I can do is tell simple stories." If you can tell good stories, if you can communicate with your whole person the power of an experience, that's great. Stories are the things people remember. The Jesuit retreat master Anthony de Mello once described theology as "the art of listening to and telling stories about God." That's a one-sentence definition of story theology. He also defined "mysticism" as the art of being transformed by such stories.

When I recorded my first set of audiocassettes on Scripture, I shared a lot of ideas and thoughts, but only a few stories, one of which was "The Flying Carpet and the Stone Table." As it turned out, that story had much more power than most of my abstract teachings. Today, when I give retreats and lectures, people still ask me to retell the story of the flying carpet.

Why does a story have such power? Because most of us don't think abstractly. We live in a world of images and symbols; that's what moves us. That's the way God most deeply created us. Elie Wiesel in *The Gates of the Forest*, wrote, "God made humans because God loves stories."

Each of us is a story. We were created by God as a story waiting to be told, and each of us has to find a way to tell our story. In the telling of it we come to recognize and own ourselves. People without a place to tell their story and a person to listen to it never come into possession of themselves.

Wiesel tells the following parable, which I am relating as I remember it:

> When the city was in trouble, Rabbi Israel Balshem would retreat to a certain place in the forest to light a fire and say a prayer, and the misfortune that was upon his people would be avoided. After this first rabbi died, this task fell to a second rabbi, who knew both the place in the forest and the prayer, but did not know the ritual for lighting the fire. Nevertheless, he did what he could and the misfortune was avoided. A third rabbi knew only the place; but forgot the prayer and how to make the fire. But this too was enough and the misfortune was

avoided. Generations later, the task fell to a rabbi who knew neither the place, nor the fire, nor the prayer. He simply remembered the story. All he could do was feel a deep compassion for his people and tell them the story. And this was sufficient to avert the misfortune.

In fact, Wiesel might say, telling the story as your story — or the story of your people — has tremendous power in itself.

With our objectified sacramental theology, it is very easy for Catholics to get involved in doing everything "right" (either in a liberal or a conservative mode), and sometimes we forget to walk in the mystery of the story. We claim to own the gospel story, but we don't know how to tell it anymore because the story is not really our own. We may say it belongs to us, but it really doesn't. It is not who we are. We are not a part of it. It is a story that others have told us, and we merely repeat it. Unlike the last rabbi, we don't tell the gospel story full of compassion for our people, wanting to help them out of their misfortune. We don't make the story our own. We recite it — perhaps even clearly and dramatically — but it is not who we are.

A few months ago I was at a well-put-together anniversary liturgy. You could tell the celebrants and ministers understood ritual and had a good sense of music. The liturgy was perfectly composed. And yet I realized there was no "fire" in it, no freedom, no union, no communion, no peace. It wasn't working. The thought that came to mind was, "These good people have come together — clergy and religious — with the best of intentions and talents. What they are mostly experiencing is someone else's experience of Jesus." They were using all the right words — they were skilled, charismatic, if you will; the right songs were being sung — but they were celebrating someone else's story. Obviously, it wasn't their story. They were taking words out of someone else's mouth. The right words, but not their words.

Our Mythology

For many people, myth means something that isn't true. Please put aside that understanding. That's not the way I'm using the word. And that's not the historical meaning either. Myth is, in fact, something that is so true that it can be adequately expressed only in story, symbol, and ritual. It can't be abstracted and objectified. Its meaning and mystery are so deep and broad that they can be presented only in story form. When you step into a story, you find it is without limits and you can walk around with it and inside it. It is natural to sing, dance, and reenact a story. It is too big and too deep to be merely "understood" or taught. It is a big truth.

Every coming together of people has to have its myth. A myth is something that's personal, shared, experiential. It begins with collective dreaming and envisioning, and, perhaps most important of all, it becomes collective remembering. For people who have a shared history, there's nothing more powerful than remembering.

I recall an evening when a group of us were doing just that. We were retelling our New Jerusalem myth; to us members it is a very powerful community story. We recalled the events of seven years before that first pulled us together. In the remembering, something rich, deep, and good happened. Some newer community people, who weren't a part of those first days, asked us original members to tell the originating story — the powerful things that happened during our first days as the Spirit pulled us together: the sense of the presence of God, the miracles, the healings, the gift of the mansion. They wanted to know the names of the young men attending the retreat that began the community. "What was it like? Are they still around?" Original members who still live in the New Jerusalem community carry a special aura about them. They experienced the community myth first-hand. Newcomers say to them reverently, "You were there in the beginning. . . . "

Today, telling stories about our past is often called a "nostalgia trip," but there's something very powerful about people remembering what they did together or what people they loved did together. Children often ask questions of their parents. "When and where did you meet? What was your dating like?" The young people are trying to discover their roots, and only their parents carry the story of their origins. They want to know how they came into existence.

The phenomenon of *Roots* is exactly that: the Afro-American people finding out their myth. If you don't know your myth, if you don't know the symbol system out of which you came, you don't know who you are. You really don't. It is important to understand this. That's the reason for the Hebrew fascination with genealogies.

The Jews understood why Matthew and Luke presented genealogies of Jesus. They believed you have to know your parents and your grandparents in order to know yourself. Moreover, to know things about your parents and grandparents can be a great healing gift. I don't know exactly why that's true; it's sort of nonrational, but it certainly is true.

For example, I found out recently that my old grandmother used to pray the Rosary six times a day. That discovery grounded me in a most amazing way. Just knowing that fact, I felt much holier! I felt I was on solid spiritual ground because my grandmother said six Rosaries a day. Why? There's nothing rational about it. But now I know that quality of prayer is somehow in my genes. I may say to myself, "A little bit of that spirit of prayer may have rubbed off on me. Maybe that's who I am. I guess holiness runs in my family."

We all want to discover things like that in our biological backgrounds. There's a tremendous power and goodness in it. And if we don't, we are certainly "orphaned." The biblical word for not knowing your roots is not "orphan," but "bastard." The word implies that, without knowing our roots, we're not truly related; we're not truly connected; we're alienated, which is the case with much of our society today.

Several years ago I was invited to preach the homily at my own ancestors' hundredth anniversary in the United States. The reason my great-great-grandparents came over to America was because they wouldn't fight for Russia in the 1860s. In studying a book published on our people, I found out they came to the United States as cultural pacifists. This was quite a discovery. They came to America looking for land approximately like their own where they could farm in peace. They located an area of western Kansas that was much like their farmland in Germany, so they settled there. If you go to western Kansas you will see the big Cathedral of the Plains, many other large churches, and an entire set of little villages where my ancestors all came from, on both my mother's and father's sides.

In a hundred years time, that original group of "draft dodgers" produced four hundred religious sisters, a hundred priests, and two bishops. I was deeply honored to be selected to give the homily to this group. In preparing for the homily, I thought, "This is a perfect chance to proclaim our original family myth, the pacifist myth of our good German-American ancestors."

I must mention that, when the Second World War began, all the Germans — at least those in Kansas — felt ashamed of being German. (Born in 1943, I wasn't even taught to speak German because the language apparently reminded them of their shame.) So all my uncles went off to war to prove they were superpatriotic Americans. In many ways, they terminated the original myth of the people gathered together on that day. When in my sermon I reminded them that their great grandparents were — I shouldn't have used this word — "draft dodgers," they didn't want to remember. (This is one audiotape I made that has fortunately *not* been duplicated.)

In the church, we have a Catholic myth and a powerful symbol system. "Holy Mother Church" is a part of all those raised in the Catholic Church before Vatican II. Even though some would rather not remember that myth, the symbol of Holy Mother Church deeply touches us still. Even with all the theology I've had that tends to put the Holy Mother symbol aside, when I'm in a little town watching a May procession, something deep happens inside me.

We were raised on those symbols. They spoke to us as little kids, and they remain a part of us forever. Like seeing religious sisters in full habits. We're all glad sisters no longer have to wear them, but at the same time there was something beautiful about it. And we'd be lying to deny it. We loved to see those long black habits. In many ways, these mother-figures who taught us and raised us gave us a feeling of security. For us, all that black wasn't a symbol of evil, but a symbol of good. It meant: Protection, Stability, the Latin Mass, the Saints.

When the winds of renewal came with Vatican II, that Catholic myth and its symbol system were almost blown away overnight. We returned to a biblical myth. We really did, but almost no one knew what had happened.

In today's church, we're not abandoning our mythology. We're returning to our original mythology. Although it may seem unfamiliar to us, it is really totally traditional. While Holy Mother Church mythology was mainly a devotional mythology, our original mythology was biblical. The Exodus myth summarizes the Hebrew Scriptures and the Jesus myth summarizes the Christian Scriptures. Those are the two big symbol systems — the Exodus story and the Jesus story. Those are the stories we're being called to appropriate, that is, to make our own.

We're being called to experience what it means to cross the Red Sea and to journey from Egypt to Israel, from slavery to freedom. Each of needs to experience that freedom the Hebrews felt. Somehow, to be a good Christian you've got to walk Exodus and become a good Jew first.

What Biblical Scholars Say

For what I say in the following pages about Luke's Gospel, I have to depend on biblical scholars. I'm not really a scholar, but a popularizer. That is our Franciscan charism. Here are some conclusions I see the scholars giving us: Luke probably composed the infancy narrative — his first two chapters — from beginning to end, much like composers who start with a blank sheet of music paper wanting to communicate what they hear in their head and heart. Luke was not taking his stories from newspaper accounts, for there weren't any newspapers. Neither was he drawing from material in books about Jesus' infancy and childhood, for there were none. In writing his gospel, Luke crafted the first two chapters around some items of information about Jesus' birth and some stories being handed down in the popular tradition, much like a composer might craft a beautiful sonata around a few popular traditional melodies.

Because of this, as we get into chapters 1 and 2, I'm going to be discussing some of your favorite nativity stories, ones you grew up with, and I will be saying, "Luke made up that story." And, just as my relatives resented me when I told them our original German immigrant families were pacifists, some of you are going to resent me. "Are you taking that beautiful story away from me, saying it isn't true?" I'm not taking the story away. I hope I'm giving it back to you.

People like to find what's behind the words, but I'd like to turn that around and ask, "What's in front of the words?" What world can these words open up for me? To me, that's more important than what's hidden behind the words. What new perspective can the gospel open up to us if we really understand storytelling?

The infancy narrative serves as a transition from the Hebrew Scriptures to the gospels. That's why Luke's first two chapters, presented in the full imagery of Israel, offer a most exciting theology. Almost every verse in the infancy narrative is adapted from lines in the Hebrew Bible. For people in Luke's time, who were steeped in that Bible and understood the Jewish myth, these familiar lines were power-packed.

Centuries later, you and I, uninitiated into the Jewish myth, come along and we miss the symbolism in those first pages of Luke. We tend to read Luke's words as historical fact, as if things really happened that way. And that's not the point at all. In fact, to ask Luke for journalistic accuracy is limiting the truth that he's really trying to tell us.

Artistically, the evangelists were most free to create in this area of Jesus' birth and childhood precisely because these stories were not a part of the apostolic preaching. Stories and sayings dealing with the public life of Jesus, which the apostles had been teaching for decades, enjoyed a certain validity and authority. Everyone knew them and agreed to keep telling them in the same way. Thus, the evangelists could not be nearly as free in shaping stories about the public life of Jesus as they could stories about his birth and childhood.

We have no record that Jesus ever talked about his own childhood; we have no record that Mary ever talked about it. It used to be said that Mary and Luke were friends, and Mary told Luke all the stories we read in his gospel. Contemporary biblical scholars are no longer affirming Mary as a major source for Luke. It might be true, they admit, but the evidence that Raymond Brown gathered in *The Birth of the Messiah* would seem to say, "Not likely." Besides, Luke's development and presentation of these birth stories are so theological, clearly they are coming from a source or sources different from informal storytelling.

If you start reading the opening of Luke's Gospel in the light of the background I've given you, I think you'll be in a good position to understand it in ways you never did before. In the following chapters, I'll lead you through the Gospel of Luke. I hope it will become apparent to you how his gospel is, indeed, good news, and how its good news applies to us today.

Two

From Jesus' Birth to the Close of His Galilean Ministry

Parallel Birth Stories

"Seeing that many others have undertaken to draw up the accounts of the events that have taken place among us exactly as these were handed down to us by those who were eyewitnesses and ministers of the word, I in my turn, after carefully going over the whole story from the beginning, have decided to write an orderly account for you, Theophilus" (1:1–4). Theophilus means "Friend of God." Luke may have intended it to be a symbolic name, since he is writing to all those who love God. Of course, there might have been an individual named Theophilus, in which case the name would be both personal for the man so named and symbolic for the rest of us.

The interesting thing about this prologue is that Luke knows he is going to take liberties with the text in order to weave a faith experience around stories from the early life of Jesus. He knows he's going to shape those infancy stories in a unique way, but he is anxious to assert that everything he writes is built upon the tradition. "It's because I know the tradition that I can write an orderly account," is what he's saying here. "It's because I've been in touch with the eyewitnesses and ministers of the word that I'm able to do this." He wants to align his gospel with the apostolic tradition. He wants us to realize, "I'm a part of this myth. This is the Jesus story as I have experienced it."

I can understand what Luke is saying. Sometimes when I talk about the beginnings of the New Jerusalem Community and our myth, I feel free to tell stories and recount conversations in a way that evokes a true understanding of the community. I feel free to embroider and elaborate in ways that bring out the meaning and significance of the event. I might not quote people exactly; I can't remember exact words, but I can tell you the story of the first days of the community. I might say with great assurance, "Bill asked this question and then Mary said this," even though they probably didn't use those words at all. But I'm so in possession of the meaning and significance of that day that I can communicate it by telling that story and doing what you would call "taking liberties." Are my words a quote? No. I don't remember exactly what Bill and Mary said. But I understand the New Jerusalem myth because I am a part of its tradition, so I can talk about it with authority.

In a similar way, Luke is saying in the Prologue, "I understand the Jesus myth and I'm part of that apostolic tradition. I've been in touch with the eyewitnesses and teachers, so I'm free to talk about it. I can talk about it because I am a witness myself. I am a witness because I have stepped into the Jesus story and am living it, even though I never knew Jesus with the eyes of the flesh."

Immediately after addressing Theophilus, Luke begins the story of John the Baptist. I think it always surprises people and disturbs some that Luke highlights John the Baptist so much. Why does John deserve all this respect, getting honorable mention in all four gospels?

One reason is because, among his contemporaries, he had quite a name on the Jewish religious scene. He could claim a large following, a set of disciples, and a teaching of his own, which at first blush would seem to be, if not contrary to Jesus' teaching, certainly something emphatically different. Yet, he seemed to be ready to let go of it in a moment, and say, "I'm only the beginning of the story; Jesus is its fulfillment. Go beyond me to him."

Because John the Baptist represented a major strand of Jewish spirituality at the time, it seemed to be very important for the evangelists to compare Jesus to the Baptist and to show how the two men related to each other. Many Jews came to Christianity through the baptism of John or because they were, first of all, disciples of John, so the connection between the two was very important.

Humans are inveterate comparers. For example, if we had a good and great American president whom everybody revered (Kennedy was

beginning to be that; there was certainly a Kennedy myth), each president after him would naturally be compared to him and viewed in
relation to him. That's what the evangelists are doing. Jesus is being
compared to John and placed in relation to him. And yet they always
want to show that Jesus goes beyond John, is the fulfillment of John's
message, and John himself is all for it.

In recent church history, we saw that Pope John XXIII wanted Cardinal Montini to be elected the next pope. It was as though John XXIII
was pointing beyond himself. "I've started this radical and scary Vatican II thing in the church, and I think this man can carry it on."
So from the beginning, Pope Paul VI enjoyed an aura of authority
because everybody trusted Pope John. Anybody Pope John said was
okay was probably okay. That acknowledgment helped Pope Paul
through his hard life, poor man, trying to hold together the church
in a revolutionary era.

Similarly, it seems to me that's why John the Baptist is given so
much authority at the beginning of each gospel. He was a prophetic
spokesperson for Judaism, but was hated by many, as they hated all
the prophets. Still they knew he was a prophet. For John to say that
Jesus was the culmination of his teaching gave credence to the life
of Jesus.

What we have in these first two chapters of Luke is a series of
parallels. Luke is good at drawing parallels between two stories. For
example, those familiar with the Hebrew Scriptures would immediately see the interaction between Zachary and Elizabeth about having
a child in old age as comparable to that of Abraham and Sarah. The
couple in Luke's story are like Abraham and Sarah questioning, "How
can we have a child in our old age? This is impossible." That dialogue
establishes Zachary in the Abraham tradition of Israel.

But there is another, more important parallelism for Luke. The
narrative in which the birth of John the Baptist is first announced parallels — almost step by step — the annunciation scene where Jesus'
birth is foretold. Here's the sequence of parallels: First the angel
Gabriel comes to Zachary (see 1:19), then the same angel comes to
Mary (1:26). Second, when the angel appears, Zachary is startled
(1:12) and so is Mary (1:29). Third, the angelic message to each is
much the same: to Zachary it is *"Do not be afraid, Elizabeth will
bear you a son, you will call his name John"* (1:13). To Mary it is,
"Mary, you are the highly favored one. Do not be afraid, you will

conceive and give birth to a son and you will name him Jesus" (1:31). Next, the angel says to Zachary, *"He will be great before the Lord"* (1:14); to Mary, *"He will be great"* (1:32). Again, they ask the angel the same question: Zachary asks, *"How am I to know this?"* (1:18) and Mary asks, *"How can this be?"* (1:34). Then, the angel's response is to give them each a sign from God — something only God could do: to Zachary it is *"Behold you will be reduced to silence"* (1:20); to Mary it is the virginal conception (1:35).

Thanks to another parallel story in the Hebrew Scriptures, people reading Luke's Gospel would recognize Zachary being struck dumb by God as a traditional sign rather than primarily a punishment. In the Book of Daniel, recall Daniel's interaction with the angel Gabriel. When the angel Gabriel appeared to Daniel, the prophet didn't believe the angel's message and he was struck dumb (see Dan. 8:15–19). In crafting this nativity story as a transition from the Old to the New Testament, Luke implies the parallelism between Zachary and Daniel.

Mary's response to the divine sign goes beyond Zachary's. It is a response of perfect acceptance (1:38), and the angel goes away happy. Mary trusts. She goes beyond Daniel and Zachary, just as the Second Testament goes beyond the First. Zachary emerges from his encounter with the angel in the temple dumb and unable to speak, and goes back home (1:23). Mary goes from her home in faith and love to serve her cousin Elizabeth (1:39). During Mary's visit to Elizabeth, the older woman, filled with the Holy Spirit, proclaims praise of the Mother of the Lord (1:41–45). Passing on the glory, Mary, inspired by the Spirit, praises God for the wonderful things God has done to her (1:46–55).

This continual parallelism is one of the strong signs that we are dealing here with a beautifully crafted story put together by a master storyteller and theologian for people who understand the Jewish myth.

There are still more parallels in these two annunciation accounts. Both infants will bring joy and delight: The angel tells Zachary, "He will be your joy, your delight, and many will rejoice at his birth" (1:14). In the Jesus story, the angels and shepherds rejoice at his birth (2:10–20). Both children will have great destinies: John will be great in the sight of the Lord; he must drink no wine or strong drink (1:15). This is foretelling the destiny of John to become the ascetic prophet. "Even from his mother's womb John will be filled with the Holy Spirit" (1:16). Luke is saying: "From the very beginning, John the Baptist was protected by the Lord."

Note Luke's appreciation of the Holy Spirit. From the very first chapter and throughout his gospel, whenever he can involve the Holy Spirit, he does it.

"With the Spirit and power of Elijah, he will go before him, to turn the hearts of fathers toward their children" (1:17). That's a famous line in the Hebrew prophetic writings, found in the conclusion of the Book of Malachi. In our listing, his are the very last words of the Hebrew Scriptures. In the *Tanakh,* or Hebrew listing, Malachi is the last prophetic book. In either case, the connection or nexus between the Hebrew and Christian Testaments is clearly made with John the Baptist as the "Elijah reborn." He reconnects the eldering system through a brilliant and healing quote about fathers and children: "In the last days, the Lord will send Elijah the prophet and he will turn the eyes of fathers toward their children and children toward their father and if this does not happen, the land will be struck with a curse" (Mal. 3:23–24).

Luke is telling his readers, "John is that prophet, the new Elijah who is going to show people how to be reconciled." Luke sees John as the prophet who is to reconcile those who are alienated, broken, divided, and separated one from another. Luke presents John as a healer, doing what we would call today "inner healing." He's going to teach fathers and children how to be reconciled. If this doesn't happen, the people will never be prepared for Jesus.

Reconciliation with Fathers

I find myself frequently teaching reconciliation between fathers and their children. Many people have had bad experiences with their fathers, and until that's redeemed and freed, until they experience reconciliation with their fathers, or healing from the wounds of that father relationship, it is very hard — if not impossible — for such people to experience the loving, reconciling fatherhood of God.

That's part of the reason why so many people have found it much easier to relate to Mary than to the Father or Jesus. In their human experience these believers have had no warm male authority figure in life they could trust; they found it was much easier to believe in the warm loving mother, Mary.

Because we operate out of symbols and images, we're not as logical and rational as we'd like to believe. Not at all. For many people in relating to God, Mary, the woman symbol, is much more believable and attractive than even the Jesus symbol, because of their bad experience of maleness. Unfortunately, those bad experiences of maleness and fatherhood are on the increase.

Malachi the prophet was talking about what happens when children can't relate to their fathers: "When that happens, the land is struck with a curse" (Mal. 3:24). When the eldering system breaks down, the male is no longer able to trust or entrust himself to anybody, and the female is no longer able to trust the male or entrust herself to the male. At that point, people have a distorted and restricted view of the nature of themselves, one another, and God. This is our cultural state today. Robert Bly rightly calls it "a sibling society," needing but rejecting all mentoring. I wish more people were dealing with holistic liberation instead of simply focusing on men's or women's liberation. We need one another; maleness and femaleness are the absolutely necessary complements.

The Mary symbol in the church is far more important than many have been ready to admit. I'm not saying Mary is God. But at the same time, her assumption to such a high level in the divine plan seems to be God's symbolic way of communicating to us the importance of the feminine. In our old theological language, Mary was called the Mediatrix, the way to the Father. On a psychological level, it's true that the feminine gives us a special access to God. God does not need Mary's help in relating to us, but because of our wounded relationship to the male we need her help psychologically in relating to God.

In praying for healing for people who cannot access the masculine or have been wounded by the feminine, I find it important to invoke Mary. In this way, Mary becomes a mediator for them. Through Mary, through the feminine symbol, they can release themselves to God. That's what calling Mary "mediatrix of grace" is saying *psychologically.* God uses images to mediate life and healing.

Christians who don't understand the psychological necessity of Mary just react by saying, "It's bad theology; you Catholics overdo it." Yes, Catholics have overdone it. I don't deny it, but don't throw out the baby with the bath water. If we throw out Mary, we've lost the sense of something familial, personal, whole, and alive in our theology. Catholicism has seen itself symbolically much more as community and family (Holy Mother Church, fathers, sisters, brothers, meal as a central symbol, etc.), whereas Protestantism, being more verbal, seems to have lost the imagery of family. Psychologically, when you lose the

mother, you lose the sense of family. That's where both the Hebrew
and Christian Scriptures are coming from. Luke recognized that the
Jesus story is rooted in eldering, motherhood, and family. These are
critical to the entire infancy narrative.

Anawim Spirituality

Zachary said to the angel, *"How can I be sure of this? I am an old
man and my wife is getting on in years"* (1:18).

The angel replies, *"I am Gabriel, who stands in God's presence. I
have been sent to speak to you and give you this good news. But since
you have not believed..."* (1:19–20). Like Sarah and Abraham, he
can't believe the impossible, whereas Mary can.

Barrenness and fruitfulness are the very basics of life. We experience
ourselves as barren and impotent; then God comes into our sterile existence and creates new life. Throughout Hebrew history and now into
the Christian era, God is making the barren fruitful. That's what Luke
is saying in this story; it's much more than a simple historical account.
Maybe Elizabeth was, in fact, barren; but that's not what Luke is trying to tell us here. He's saying, "We're all symbolically barren women
who of ourselves cannot bring forth life into the world, but by the
overshadowing of the Holy Spirit we will bring forth the prophet."

God has to go one step further with Mary — and with us. She
was not barren, she was virginal. Whether we need healing or full
transformation, God becomes the gift-giver. Continuing the biblical
pattern that starts with Exodus, Yahweh always turns death into life,
emptiness into fullness, barrenness into fertility, and, in Mary's case,
humanity into divinity.

Elizabeth goes into seclusion for five months. *"The Lord has done
this for me,"* she says. *"Now he has ended the humiliation I suffered
among others"* (1:25). It is to this "women's pregnancy shelter" that
Mary will travel to be with Elizabeth. I have visited the spot in Ain
Karim (to give a Franciscan retreat), and I think we need to rediscover
such support systems for pregnant women.

Now that we are ready, Luke presents *the* annunciation scene so
familiar to us. If you have a scholarly Bible or student edition, note
the cross references and marginal notes in this section. The announcement is a gathering from any number of Hebrew scriptural passages:
Psalms, Isaiah, Daniel, Judith. For almost every line in the annunciation, there is a Hebrew Scripture reference. One of the most significant

of those references is Zephaniah 2:3; 3:11–13. It is the spirituality out of which Luke is presenting Mary: "Seek Yahweh, all you, the humble of the earth [anawim], who obey his commands. Seek integrity, seek humility; you may perhaps find shelter on the day of the anger of Yahweh" (Zeph. 2:3).

The word *anawim* means "the little poor ones," a term we are growing to appreciate in twentieth-century theology. According to this spirituality, God is raising up a poor people, a meek people, who shall possess the earth. These little ones, the poor broken people, the remnant, somehow become the purest sign of receptivity to God (see Luke 6:20–23).

In Jesus' day, there was a school of spirituality — just like we'd speak of Franciscan or Jesuit spirituality — called the *anawim*. There was another school called *Qumran* spirituality, characteristic of the Essene groups that came out of the desert, with whom John the Baptist might have been associated. In his public life John represents Qumran spirituality, the ascetic spirituality of the desert. Mary represents anawim spirituality; she is the little poor woman, the "forgettable" remnant with which God will do something new.

To give you a sense of this, I will read from Zephaniah: "In your midst I will leave a humble and lowly people. Those who are left in Israel will seek refuge in the name of Yahweh. . . . They will be able to graze and rest and no one will disturb them" (Zeph. 3:12–13). It is an image of a people of peace, people who are quiet, receptive, humble and poor, as opposed to great thinkers, warriors, royalty, or people of position.

Then he breaks forth in verse 14: "Shout for joy, daughter of Zion. Israel shout out loud, rejoice and exult with all your heart, Daughter of Jerusalem" (Zeph. 3:14). Mary is the summation of Israel. She is Israel prepared for two thousand years — one woman, one person who sums up Jewish spirituality. She is the virgin/mother, physical impossibility but spiritual pattern. It is henceforth clear that we bring to God our *emptiness* (virginity) as opposed to our fullness and fertility. It is the barren and the virgins (the *anawim*) who become mothers, not the perfect and the self-made. It is a "spirituality of imperfection" as opposed to our modern philosophy of progress.

"Yahweh has repealed your sentence, he has driven your enemies away. Yahweh, your king, is in your midst" (Zeph. 3:15). The Hebrew phrase "in your midst" is the same phrase exactly as "in your womb." "You have no more evil to fear. When that day comes, word will come to Jerusalem, 'Have no fear, Zion, do not let your hands fall limp, Yahweh, your God is in your midst [in your womb]. A victorious warrior. He will exult with joy over you, he will renew you by his love. He will dance with shouts of joy as on a day of festival' " (Zeph. 3:16–18).

If you catch the sexual/spiritual/ecstatic metaphors, you'll get a sense of the beauty and power of the *anawim* spirituality. It lays a firm foundation for a spirituality, not of perfection but of imperfection, not of wholeness but of emptiness and need. This insight will be lost to much of Christianity, but it will be rediscovered from time to time by the likes of Augustine, Francis of Assisi, the Little Flower, and now in the spirituality of Alcoholics Anonymous. How wonderful that Mary herself is a primary icon of this tradition. The little one is the fruitful one.

Luke 1: The Coming of Jesus

"The angel Gabriel was sent by God" (1:26). Luke has Gabriel the angel make the announcement. An angel is primarily an experienced presence of God. Since God, for the Jewish mind, was so totally beyond us, God simply could not appear or be present physically in the physical world, so God communicated through a messenger. Angels were considered emanations from God, the presence of God in space and time. In this story Luke is using the word "angel" simply to mean "One who carries the message of God."

"He went in and said to her, 'Rejoice, O highly favored one, the Lord is with you' " (1:28). In the "Hail Mary" prayer, we say "full of grace," but the Greek word that Luke used means "favored to the greatest possible degree." It was the strongest word Luke could use to show how much God loved Mary and prepared her.

"And Mary was greatly troubled" (1:29). Her response, understandably, was to be deeply disturbed by these words. Whenever a person in the Scriptures encounters the Holy, the transcendent, God, the response is always one of awesome fear. That's universal. A predominant emotion in the Scriptures is fear — and especially fear of God. But God is constantly calling us beyond that fear. In the Bible, the opposite of faith is not doubt, because faith has not yet been re-

duced to an intellectual problem. The opposite of faith seems usually to be anxiety or "worrying about many things" (see Luke 12:22ff.).

One could sum up the Bible as an interplay of fear and faith. In general, people are obsessed and overpowered by fears; they fear what they cannot control. God is one of our primary fears, because God is totally beyond us, totally immense, and totally beyond our control. Realizing we are nothing in comparison to God, we are scared. The good news is that the Lord has breached that fear and become one of us in Jesus. God says, in effect, "You can stop being afraid. It's okay. You don't have to live in chattering fear of Me." God's response to Mary, through the angel, is *"Do not be afraid"* (1:30).

In this infancy narrative, Mary is presented as the prototypical Christian, the archetypal Christian, the summary Christian, because God comes into her life and announces the divine presence within her. She is the prototype for us because, through the same divine Spirit, God comes into our lives and announces the divine presence within us. This annunciation event is a paradigm of every baptism in the Spirit. God offers Godself to us even before we invite God into our lives. All we are asked to do is be present and open. When Mary manifests this presence and openness, God enters her, praising her, believing in her, inviting her!

How many of you could tell a similar story of your baptism in the Spirit? Probably many of you. God baptized you almost against your will. You were hardly present to God, hardly open, hardly asking for it. It was obviously God's initiative, obviously God's invitation and gift. That's what we see modeled here in Mary.

"Mary, do not be afraid" (1:30). He then proceeds to give her the message, but only after he has called her beyond fear. It seems that fear can keep us from hearing what is really being said. Religion can easily become our projecting ourselves onto reality instead of remaining receptive and open before reality, letting it speak to us. Receptivity is the favored attitude in Scripture. Listening seems to be more important than speaking. We have to get out of the way to make room for what is.

"Slick" Christianity builds on some of the worst American personality types and temperaments. The admired American personality is the "go-getter," the overachiever, the spiritual jogger. We don't recognize our own system of values; in fact, we bring that whole system to our prayer — our way of overachieving, overdoing, oversucceeding.

Before we are human doers, we must be human beings. Mary is a prototype here.

Luke's Gospel, first of all, calls us to "being," to enter into who-we-are more than what-we-do. Any "doing" you do as a Christian will naturally and spontaneously come out of your being, but the being has to be deeply realized within you first.

St. Francis told us. "The primary apostolate of the Friars Minor is simply to *live* the gospel life in simplicity and joy." That's our ministry! In another place he said, "Preach the gospel at all times, and when necessary use words." You might say, "That's no ministry," but Francis said it was. He told us, "You have been set free to live the gospel in simplicity and joy."

That's the greatest good news. It becomes healing for others when they encounter a new kind of human synthesis, a true alternative to the predictable human response. Someone who *is* the answer instead of someone who just talks about the answer. It is not a competing religion as much as a truthful lifestyle that we need.

It is good that we have contemplative ("useless") communities like the Trappists and the Poor Clares. It is only the Whole Church that is Christ's Body. Each of us represent certain parts or functions of that Body. Some represent Christ in the desert, others Christ healing, others Christ preaching. If we didn't have contemplatives at one end of the spectrum, we would not represent the whole of Christ. Contemplatives pull all of us back to some kind of midpoint, to balance the overachiever Christianity at the other end. "The eye cannot say to the hand, 'I do not need you' " (1 Cor. 12:21).

Luke does not present Mary as an evangelizing activist. Mary is merely living a simple and good life. As such, she is the model of the contemplative Christian. She doesn't do anything special. She's a good mother and she listens to her God. According to the historical accounts we have, she didn't evangelize anybody, yet obviously her life was totally good news for the world. Please hear Luke's message on this point and tell it to people who need to find some kind of balance. It calls us all to a new integrity.

Historically, the great apostles and activists have been the great contemplatives. Their message to us is, "Don't just do something — stand there!" Learn to listen and wait upon the Lord. Amazingly, out of that receptivity, God brings the greatest energy and activity. That may seem a paradox, but it has been the Christian experience throughout our tradition. The greatest apostles began by being the greatest listeners and be-ers. Already in the first century of the church, Luke recognized this paradox and gave it flesh in Mary.

"*Mary said to the angel, 'How can this come about, since I am a virgin?'* " (1:34) In the original Greek, "since I am a virgin" best reads, "I have not had relations with a man." She's just being very practical. Mary knew the facts of life, so she asks the angel bluntly, "Since I have not had sexual relations, how can I have a child?" It is not a question of disbelief, but a set-up question for the necessary explanation.

And Gabriel obliges, "*The Holy Spirit will come upon you and the power of the Most High will cover you with its shadow*" (1:35). Here is a clear allusion to the Hebrew Scriptures. How is the Lord present in their biblical books? Again and again as the cloud, overshadowing now the Ark of the Covenant, now the temple, now the chosen people. Luke is presenting Mary as the New Ark of the Covenant, the New Temple, and the first of the New People, surrounded, overshadowed, and penetrated by the presence of God. A magnificent metaphor for the divine conception.

All humankind is feminine before God, it seems. This has been a recurring theme in both mystic and poetic literature, although sometimes resisted by contemporary feminist thought. The theme is presented in powerful imagery in a poem by "Brother Antoninus":

> Annul in me my manhood, Lord, and make
> Me women-sexed and weak,
> If by that total transformation
> I might know Thee more.
> What is the worth of my own sex
> That the bold possessive instinct
> Should but shoulder Thee aside?
> What uselessness is housed in my loins,
> To drive, drive, the rampant pride of life,
> When what is needful is a hushed quiescence?
> "The soul is feminine to God,"
> And hangs on impregnation,
> Fertile influxing Grace. But how achieve
> The elemental lapse of that repose,
> That watchful, all-abiding silence of the soul,
> In which the Lover enters to His own,

Yielding Himself to her, and her alone?
How may a man assume that hiddenness of heart
Being male, all masculine and male,
Blunt with male hunger?

    Make me then
Girl-hearted, virgin-souled, woman-docile, maiden-meek;
Cancel in me the rude compulsive tide
That like an angry river surges through,
Flouts off Thy soft lip-touches, froth-blinds
The soul-gaze from its very great delight,
Outbawls the rare celestial melody.
Restless I churn. The use of sex is union,
Union alone. Here it but cleaves,
Makes man the futile ape of God, all ape
And no bride, usurps the energizing role, inverts;
And in that wrenched inversion caught
Draws off the needer from his never-ending need, diverts
The seeker from the Sought.*

This is anawim and Marian spirituality at its best, and so I had to quote it in full.

"*Know this, too: Your kinswoman has herself conceived a son, and is now in her sixth month, for nothing is impossible to God*" (1:36–37). That is the great punch line to which Luke has been building up. In the spirituality of the *anawim*, nothing is impossible to God. It is a spirituality of trusting in God, not trying to do it all yourself. Both a barren women and a virgin are now pregnant!

Mary's spirituality is focused on trusting. "Let God do with me what God will. Through my receptivity to God, my listening to God, and my surrender to God, God will achieve the divine purpose, God will do God's activity upon the earth." The statement "I am the little maidservant of the Lord" would tell any Jew of Luke's day, "This is *anawim* spirituality." It would be like me saying to you today, "I am like the Little Flower of Jesus." And you would immediately say, "Oh, he's into Carmelite spirituality."

---

*Brother Antoninus, "Annul in Me My Manhood," from *The Crooked Lines of God* (University of Detroit Press, 1962), 86.

She said, *"Let what you have said be done to me"* (1:38). She doesn't try to explain or understand, she just says, "I trust you, God. Do with me what you will. Let it be."

A Great Mystery

What we can say is Mary was the recipient of a great internal mystery, and to surrender herself to it took almost total faith. Luke's words are trying somehow to capture that mystery. She could not, with her human consciousness, have fully known or imagined what was really going on. It was unthinkable for Judaism and unthinkable for a simple, uneducated Jewish to girl to believe that she was going to hold Yahweh's child, the God of Israel, in her womb. Any Jew would have said to her, "How are you going to be able to spank Yahweh's child when he is a bad little boy?" She would have had terrible theological problems in changing a diaper! How can a divine child have bodily functions like everybody else? Truly, she also had to grow in wisdom, age, and grace.

But the text is certainly saying, and Luke is certainly saying, that whatever the mystery was, Mary was the choice of God, and by every standard she was an extraordinary person. For God, she was the culmination of all open humanity coming together in one bit of feminine flesh. Humanity, like the earth itself, is always feminine before God, always in the position of receiving the seed.

In this context, the Holy Spirit is seen as the impregnator, and Mary is seen as the eternal feminine, the earth-mother, a human consciousness who, finally in a woman's body, reaches a point where it can utter a perfectly free "yes," without any self-interest, pressure, expectations or obligations, without any kinds of shoulds or oughts. Just a full, conscious "yes." She says, in effect, "I don't know what it will mean, I don't know where it will lead, I don't know what it will require, but I know God is asking it of me, and I say a wholehearted Yes to God."

I think that's why this woman, Mary, has been so utterly loved in Catholic consciousness. Somehow she is calling all of us to our absolute best. And it's important to realize she does it through the feminine image. We know God is not masculine, not a man. But out of the patriarchal history, where Jesus himself addressed God as his Father, as Abba or Daddy, using masculine words, most people in the West at least have tended to see God as masculine.

Therefore it is utterly important that we have feminine images or icons of the divine. Not that Mary is divine; I'm not saying that. But I am saying that I can understand how she became the symbolic point of mediation between heaven and earth — the earth-mother, as it were, receiving the divine, standing in between heaven and earth. It is important because many of us can trust feminine love more easily than we can trust love through masculine imagery. Today in America 47 percent of children are being raised without a full-time father, or with no father at all.

Mary is the woman who goes inside, beyond the contradictions and absurdities, to treasure and hold the mystery until she finally embraces the paradox. As she learns to deal with the contradictions in the outer world, she can learn to deal with the mystery of God's holiness. In that she calls us all to our contemplative vocation to trust and, ironically, to have absolute radical faith.

At the very end of the gospel, this same gentle feminine trusting woman is presented at the foot of the cross. Even though almost all the apostles have run away, there she is, faithfully standing beside him. She achieves understanding by treasuring the mystery in her heart, and it leads her to identifying with her son.

Remember how uneducated she is, how simple she is, how unprepared she is, humanly speaking, for her son to question the State and challenge the established religion. Imagine how hard that was for her. I know how hard it was for my mother, when she started listening to my first audiotapes! She said to me, in effect, "Come home and spend Sunday afternoons with me, and don't talk about these things." Mothers always want their boys to be "nice," a credit to the family. I'm sure Mary did too.

Finally, Mary is not only a contemplative, but also engaged with what life presents to her. Having such an extraordinary visit from an angel, you would think her reaction might be, "Oh, my God, I need a thirty-day retreat to comprehend all this." And what does she do? The next verse tells us, *"Mary set out as quickly as possible to a town in the hill country of Judah"* (1:39). There you see her balance. She's a contemplative, but immediately her contemplation leads her to action. You'd think she'd be preoccupied with herself and her greatness. "Oh my God, what am I going to wear?!" Instead, as soon as she heard the announcement, she was free enough from self-preoccupation to concern herself with her cousin who was already pregnant, and she wished to go help her.

The Visitation

After Luke has presented the annunciation of John the Baptist and the annunciation to Mary, he needs to tie these two stories together, so he has Mary set out to visit her cousin Elizabeth. It's quite a journey from Nazareth to Ain Karim. Mary would have to walk or ride a donkey for some days through very rugged and mountainous terrain. Mary's visit might well have happened historically. I'm not saying it didn't. But Luke is relating the visitation story because it is very important for his own theological purposes. Remember, Luke's community was probably a missionary center.

When Mary came into Elizabeth's presence, the older woman gave a loud cry and said, *"Of all women, you are the most blessed, and blessed is the fruit of your womb."* (1:42) This is almost a direct quote from the Hebrew Bible, the Book of Judith. After killing Holofernes, the enemy of the Jewish people, Judith — just an ordinary woman — returns to her community, and the people say, "You are the most blessed of all women" (Jud. 13:23). Luke uses that line of praise given to Judith, a great heroine in the Hebrew tradition, to characterize Mary. In doing so, Luke affirms that she is following in the tradition of Judith — a woman who, by trusting God, destroys the enemy of God's people. This passage is also where we get the words for the "Hail Mary" prayer. I know some people don't like our Hail Mary, but most of the words in the first part of the prayer are straight from Luke's Gospel.

"Why should I be honored by a visit from the mother of my Lord? From the moment your greeting reached my ear, the child in my womb leaped for joy" (1:43–44). Some scholars say that, for Luke, Mary is the new Ark of the Covenant. In King David's time, when the Ark was brought into the temple, David leaped for joy and danced around the Ark. Now in similar fashion, Luke portrays Mary coming forth as the Ark of the Covenant, and he has John the Baptist, the new prophet, leaping for joy — although still in his mother's womb.

Mary becomes the first missionary to take Christ out into the world. As if in anticipation of Pentecost, Luke has John the Baptist, even before he is born, baptized in the Holy Spirit, receiving the gift of the Spirit and jumping up and down in his mother's womb.

I hope you've had the experience of praying over women who are pregnant. When I place my hand on their stomach, often the baby will start kicking. You realize there's a transfer of spiritual energy. When you lay your hands on the child and pray with love and care, "Lord, even before its birth, fill this child with your Holy Spirit," sometimes at the very word "Holy Spirit" you can feel the kicking.

"Blessed is she who believed that the promise made her by the Lord would be fulfilled" (1:45). Again, it is the *anawim* spirituality of trusting the Lord's promises and waiting for those promises to be fulfilled. For Luke, the first disciple is a woman. No one else believes yet, no one even knows. Elizabeth proclaims, in effect, "You are the first and perfect disciple. You have said yes to him, you have carried him out into the world, you have allowed him to be an instrument of the Spirit for that world and you are the first one who believed and trusted. Blessed are you."

In Luke's Gospel as in Mark's, the women consistently come off appreciably better than the men, which suggests that this was probably the historical situation in Luke's experience and in his community.

Luke 1 and 2: Four Canticles

There are four hymns, or canticles, in Luke's infancy narrative. The Magnificat is the first (1:46–55), then the Benedictus (1:68–79), next "Glory to God in the Highest" (2:14), and finally Simeon's Nunc Dimittis (2:29–32). Why did Luke include these four hymns? Probably because each reflected a certain spirituality in the Christian church at his time, and he wanted to honor each spirituality and convey its respective emphasis to his missionaries.

The Magnificat, a beautiful hymn of divine praise, is very likely a Jewish Christian community hymn of *anawim* spirituality. So subversive is its notion of "pulling down princes . . . and exalting the lowly" that at least one Latin American government actually declared it illegal during a period of Communist threat!

The Benedictus, another hymn of praise from the Jewish Christian community, is much more Qumran spirituality — the spirituality of the desert, the spirituality that most likely influenced John the Baptist.

The third hymn, the short "Glory to God in the Highest and peace to his people on earth," is probably a refrain from a liturgical text, which Luke puts into the mouth of the angels.

Finally, Luke presents the Nunc Dimittis, a proclamation-of-destiny hymn that might have been sung in a Qumran community waiting for the coming of the Messiah, or in a Jewish Christian community waiting for the return of Jesus. Scholars also think it might have been a Christian hymn sung at funerals of those who died before Jesus' return.

But why did Luke use hymns or canticles to make his points? Because they are easier to remember. Let's say I want to communicate an experience of Jesus to you through the medium of music. I know what songs you like and I know what songs are most popular in this part of the country these days, so in telling my story of Jesus, I might pick one of the current melodies for the Magnificat, and I know that you will better remember it.

The Benedictus. is used every day at Morning Prayer and the Magnificat at Vespers. We've already put the "Glory to God" into Christmas carols, and the Nunc Dimittis is sung every night before retiring.

"Now, master, you can let your servant go in peace, it is as you promised, for my eyes have seen the salvation which you have prepared for all the nations to see, a light to enlighten the pagans and the glory of your people Israel" (2:29–32). The hymn is asking permission from God to die. That's exactly the way Simeon is using it. "God, it's okay for me to die now because I've seen the kingdom. I've seen what matters." Martin Luther King said, "I've been to the mountain top. It's okay, Lord, you can take me when you want." And the Lord took him a few weeks later.

The Magnificat

After looking at all four hymns together, you can see that Luke is creating powerful theology in these first two chapters of his gospel. Now I would like to look at the first two in more detail. The Magnificat teaches us the spirituality of the oppressed.

"My soul proclaims the greatness of the Lord
and my spirit exults in God, my savior;
because he has looked upon this little poor woman.
From this day forward all generations will call me blessed."
                                        (1:46–48)

Because of that last line, we Catholics have always spoken of Mary as the "Blessed" Mother. It's very biblical to call her blessed and to call her the Blessed Mother. It is prophesied here:

> *"All generations shall call me blessed,*
> *for the almighty has done great things for me,*
> *and holy is his name* [positive self-regard that comes from being
>   mirrored by God].
> *His mercy reaches from age to age for those who fear him*
>   [democratization of religion].
> *He has shown the power of his arm,*
> *he has routed the proud of heart* [note the great reversals],
> *he has pulled down princes from their thrones and has exalted*
>   *the lowly* [political liberation].
> *The hungry he fills with good things, the rich he sends them*
>   *empty away* [economic liberation].
> *He has come to the help of Israel, his servant, mindful of his*
>   *mercy"* [God as initiator in the relationship]. (1:46–54)

Today, in Ain Karim, a little town in the hill country, there are two churches. On one side of the village is the first, at the site of the house of Zachary and Elizabeth, where John the Baptist was born and grew up. Across the valley is the Church of the Visitation, on the site of a little house where tradition tells us Elizabeth went into hiding, which women apparently were required to do in those days. You stayed in your house totally during your months of pregnancy. That's where Mary came to visit her, as the tradition goes.

A few years ago I spent a day in that small town watching pilgrims from all over the world walk up a steep hill singing the Magnificat in dozens of languages. The amazing thing is, as soft, tender, beautiful, and lyrical as this prayer is — this prayer that Luke puts in Mary's mouth, although she might certainly have said it — it is in fact a most radical kind of prayer. For in it she talks about religious, political, social, and economic liberation. The Magnificat, this prayer of Mary, has become one of the favorite prayers of the Third World. People who are fighting for their rights and to be freed from oppression love the Magnificat. They see Mary as the truly radical Christian.

Luke has a great problem with rich Christians. It embarrasses him that there are so many rich people in the Christian community, because it means they haven't learned how to share — or they wouldn't be that rich. Whenever Luke can, he makes his point about God's love for the poor. At the same time the poverty of the *anawim* is not simply physical economic deprivation, but a vulnerability in spirit. Luke is talking about persons who are not defensive but trusting; they are disarmed persons who are open, teachable, and able to move beyond their comfort zone. *When you have power, you can change and control things; when you are powerless, you have to transform things.* This is anawim spiritual in a nutshell.

The poverty of the *anawim* is primarily spiritual poverty. But at the same time, at least in his age, Luke recognizes that it is the economically disadvantaged who are truly free to trust in God, because the rich trust in their money. The rich folk can usually buy their way out of problems, but the little guys have to trust in and call upon the Lord. This is not an either/or situation, for there are in fact people who have much money in their savings accounts and are truly living *anawim* spirituality, and there are economically deprived people who trust nobody, God included. In fact, that's the sad situation we're dealing with in First World poverty.

Poverty today is often associated with bitterness, especially in America, where a poor person grows up seeing Cadillacs drive by. When I was in the West Indies, in St. Lucia, I noticed that the poor seldom see Cadillacs, so there isn't as much bitterness associated with poverty as there is here. I'm afraid the poor in rich countries have the worst of both worlds, especially if they have lost their spiritual and cultural riches. Then there is no way out.

I'm not saying that to live in deprivation means holiness. God no doubt wants us to live well enough that we don't have to worry about survival. That's the great gift of having enough money in the bank, so we can live out the important human and personal values — the servant values — that life is all about.

But we in America have not usually used our money to free ourselves for service and for being human, for creating a meaningful family and human life. We simply use our money to provide more and more options for ourselves. That's what is hard to justify with the gospel. The gift of leisure is given — or sought — so you can be free to do the important things in life. If you become preoccupied with making your own life better — better food, a better house, a better car, better status symbols — then it seems to me you have distorted the purpose of human freedom. We need to ask what the gifts of money and commodities are for and, indeed, what *we* were created for.

Luke tells us: *"God has pulled down the princes from their thrones and will exalt the lowly. The hungry he has filled with good things, the rich he has sent empty away"* (1:52–53). God sends them away empty because they don't ask for or expect anything from God. They're already full. This verse tells us God is bringing about a horizontalization of society where there are no longer some who have the power and others who are oppressed. We are one family of God. It makes sense that these words would come from a woman, the woman who prefers the circular family to a pecking order or hierarchy. Women seem to have an intuitive preference for circles over pyramids.

If I came out and talked to you in the same spirit as Mary's Magnificat, you'd say, "Richard, you're being unfair. You've got a bias toward one side." That's the original Christian bias the church is rediscovering in our time. Today it's called the "preferential option for the poor." We see the preferential bias for the poor clearly revealed here in Mary's Magnificat. This is not new doctrine, something liberation theology invented. It's very traditional theology.

What does it mean? It means the people on the bottom of the system — any system — are usually much more ready to hear the word of God. Longing and thirsting for righteousness, they are more ready to stop protecting the status quo. Therefore they're much more ready for conversion. They have a head start, a symbolic if not real advantage.

Jesus says directly, as we'll see later on, *"I've come to preach the gospel to the poor"* (4:18). We've found, after fifteen hundred years in the Western church of trying to preach the gospel primarily to kings, princes, the rich and powerful, that the message always seemed to get prostituted. It liberates nobody: the powerful remain in their illusions and preoccupations with security; the poor remain victimized and often bitter.

We are beginning to make an important discovery. When you preach to the prisoners, to the financially poor, the handicapped, to those who are not the beneficiaries of the system — then you get a much purer response to the gospel. It is not as likely to be used and abused for the purposes of control and power. I think that's why we're only now coming to deal with Jesus' words about war and poverty. As long as we continued to preach the gospel to the people on top, it was used by them merely to support their system and worldview. They never got around to dealing with the radical questions of the gospel as found in the Magnificat.

So in the church today we speak of the bias toward the poor. We use that word "bias" intentionally. When you own your bias, then the cards are on the table. The trouble is that those enjoying the benefits of our capitalist system will seldom admit that they have a bias on the other side. "I don't have a bias," American middle-class Christians seem to say. "I just have the truth." The rationalization of power, patriarchy and free-market economics is seldom owned, because one can't see one's own shadow side.

What I've learned in middle-class America in my fifty years is that this bias toward the rich and powerful is seen as the truth and the correct view of the world. The gospel is always calling us: "Can you be converted to leave your viewpoint, to move away from your vantage point where you are the beneficiary, where you see the gospel supporting your political worldview and economic status quo, and stand in another viewpoint?" Every viewpoint is a view from a point! I'm not saying the preferential option for the poor is the whole truth, but it is an essential truth and a starting point for the gospel Jesus preached.

It's not an exclusive option, but it is a primary, preferred, and necessary one. Without including this preferential option we will read and interpret the gospels incorrectly, so they will support and maintain our bias. We call that "establishment theology" because it preserves the existing power structure. It maintains things the way they are, which is usually in support of power and control instead of truth and justice.

This current bias seems so self-evident once it's spelled out that it's amazing it has taken us so long to recognize it. If you've ever worked with poor people, you know that the people on the bottom of any system are quite aware of the establishment bias. Perhaps one of the reasons why women's religious consciousness has developed so much more quickly than men's is because women have been at the bottom of this system. People on the bottom ask different questions.

Here I am, an ordained white American male, quite comfortable and secure teaching about this establishment bias, yet I am its ultimate beneficiary. We white males control most of this planet and probably have 80 percent of the power and possessions on the earth. White, middle-class males are one of the hardest groups to preach the gospel to. Why would they want to talk about conversion and change? Why would we guys want to change anything? We're enjoying it. We've got everything. Try to talk the gospel to the people at the top. It's next to impossible.

Luke tells us that Jesus tried it a few times; with Simon the Pharisees he failed and with Zacchaeus he had some success. Most of the time in this gospel Luke just keeps preaching to the edge — to the poor, the little ones — because they are much more ready to hear the Word of God without distorting it.

The Birth of the Baptist and the Benedictus

"The time came for Elizabeth to have her child and she gave birth to a son. Neighbors and relations had heard that the Lord had shown her so great a kindness; they shared her joy" (1:57–58). Luke shows the joyful response to the birth of John the Baptist, and in the next chapter we're going to see the same joy at the birth of Jesus.

Again, Luke presents a parallelism: joyful response in both cases and circumcision of both babies. To the Jews, circumcision is comparable in importance to Christian baptism. As the Hebrew initiation rite it is very important. It's like us saying, "And he was baptized." Circumcision assures everyone the child's a part of the people of Israel in every sense. Both babies are full Jewish boys from the beginning.

Elizabeth's baby is finally given the name John. *"What will this child be?"* the people ask. *They wondered. Indeed the hand of the Lord was with him* (2:66). At this moment his father, Zachary, is filled with the Holy Spirit again. At least twenty times in his gospel Luke uses the phrase, "filled with the Holy Spirit." So now he has Zachary breaking forth in a canticle.

The Benedictus, the second canticle, is an example of Qumran spirituality. Texts of this spirituality were discovered only a short time ago, in the 1940s, when the Dead Sea scrolls were found in a wilderness section of Israel. There, scientists uncovered the archeological remains of an entire community. These scrolls spelled out some of their community rules, customs, and theology. They seemed to have been a very strict ascetic group. In a kind of apocalyptic gesture, they gave up on the corruption in Jerusalem and formed a community of righteousness in the desert.

The people of Qumran performed many rituals, especially ritual baths. Their ruins reveal many places for baths. Biblical scholars suspect that John's ritual of baptism in the River Jordan was associated with the baths of Qumran.

The Qumran community are also called the Essenes. They created many of their own symbols, especially the Son of Righteousness, symbolized as the light returning. Every morning they sat waiting for the sun. They believed that with the rising of the sun would come the Mes-

siah to free them from this wicked world. Notice the similar themes in
the Benedictus.

> "Blessed be the Lord, the God of Israel,
> for he has visited his people, he has come to their rescue,
> he has raised up for us a power for salvation
> in the House of his servant, David,
> even as he proclaimed
> by the mouth of his holy prophets from ancient times.…
> He remembers his holy covenant,
> the oath he swore to our father Abraham
> that he would grant us freedom from fear [We are always seeking
>   this freedom from fear which controls most of our lives],
> to be delivered from the hands of our enemies,
> to serve him in holiness and virtue." (2:68–74)

This is the basic Essene attitude: to go off to the desert and live a holy,
strict, and virtuous ascetic life. So the verse about John going off to the
desert and eating grasshoppers and honey could well be an allusion to
this ascetic life of the Qumran community.

> "You, little child
> you shall be called the prophet of the most high,
> you will go before the Lord to prepare his way." (2:76)

Proclaiming the destiny of this child could have been a Christian addition to the hymn's Qumran basis. In any case, naming and destiny
are important theme for Luke.

When we celebrate baptisms in our New Jerusalem community, we
like to make the event special for each infant. It's no accident, for example, that the name given is associated with the proclamation of the
child's destiny. This baptismal moment is very important because we
live the rest of our life in order to understand the meaning of our
name and the meaning of our destiny. For the Christian, baptism is
not "something"; it is "everything." Everything is given at the beginning. It takes the rest of your life to realize what was told you at your
baptism. The gift — "You are a child of God" — is given all at once,
everything at the beginning.

Your name is given at the beginning, the name you will live with
all your life. Something very deep is connoted by your name. Some

people don't like their name, especially when they are called by that name all their life.

As a child, I was always called Dickie! When I got older, I hated to be called Dickie. But my father was Richard, so what was left for me was Dickie! When my parents came to visit me at Franciscan seminary, my classmates heard them call me Dickie, so they started calling me by that name. It's a strange sounding word, but it's what I was called ever since I was a little boy. So I answer to it, and have even learned to hear its dear, remembered undertones. That's the power of a name. The rest of your life you spend learning the meaning of your name. I don't mean its etymology; I mean you learn the meaning of yourself, which that name connotes, symbolizes, and recalls if you had loving parents first speak it to you.

Notice in how many songs we sing about names: "The Lord called me by name," "Speak my name." We wait to hear our name pronounced by God. In other words, we discover our identity when God looks at us and tells us who we are. We wait for that moment when we are finally told who we are. The world doesn't tell us who we are. It denies who we are. God tells us who we really are.

> *"To give his people knowledge of salvation,*
> *through the forgiveness of their sins*
> *and by the tender mercy of our God*
> *who from on high will bring the rising Sun to visit us."*
>
> (1:77–78)

Qumran's "Rising Sun" symbol became an image of Christ. *Oriens*, the "Sun that rises," the "Orient from on high," the "Dayspring" are various ways it has been translated. The point is that the Rising Sun each day became for Christians a symbol of the Christ.

When I worked with the Indians in New Mexico as a deacon, I remember this old Indian lady telling me a lovely story:

> You know, our parents never really taught us about prayer. We didn't memorize prayers. But every morning, my mother would wake us up and, as little children, we'd have to sit on the steps of our house facing East. And she'd say, "Be quiet. You have to be quiet while you sit here. You watch the sun come up." Me and my brothers and sisters would have to sit on the steps and watch the sun rise every morning. "As the sun comes," my

mother would say to us, "welcome it. Welcome it to the world. And tell it, as it goes over the earth, it should drop its blessings on all people." That was our prayer every day.

You can claim that was a pagan kind of a prayer, but that woman is a contemplative today. She's one of those who prays eight Rosaries a day, every day. Where did her prayer life all start? She didn't enroll in a course on contemplation; her mother taught her how to watch the rising sun and make it a prayer.

When I was preaching in Puerto Rico and told that story, it surprised me when some of the young boys asked if we could get up and watch the rising sun. Next morning, we were sitting there watching the sunrise, and about half of them said they had never in their whole life seen the sun rise. We Americans watch a lot of sunsets, but most of us are never up to watch the sun rise. I'll bet some of you readers are middle-aged and you've never really watched a complete sunrise. There is something transcendent about it. Maybe it's mythological, maybe its nonrational, but somehow it's a symbol of God never giving up. If you can watch the event as God trying again, every morning putting the sun over this world, it can be a beautiful prayer experience. For those of you who can rise early, I suggest it.

> *"Who from on high will bring the Rising Sun to visit us.*
> *To give light to those who live in darkness*
> *and the shadow of death,*
> *and to guide our feet into the way of peace."* (1:79)

> *Meanwhile the child grew up and his spirit matured. And he lived out in the wilderness until the day he appeared openly to Israel.* (1:80).

It's strange that we never ask of Bible texts all the questions we'd like to ask: If you had a son, would you let him go off and live in the wilderness?

When biblical scholars begin to notice items in the text that are inconsistent, or at least not explained, those are keys that we're not talking about a historical chronological account, but that probably every line here is an important *theological* statement about the meaning of this person's life. John is *outside* the system from the beginning. Still, Luke has John growing up and maturing (1:80), and he'll say the same about Jesus: he grew in wisdom, age, and grace (see Luke 2:40, 52).

Luke 2: The Birth of Jesus and His Childhood

In chapter 2 Luke recounts the birth of Jesus and the visit of the shepherds. *"Now at this time, Caesar Augustus issued a decree"* (2:1). Actually, scholars say they can find no historical record or evidence of a census at that time. Mary and Joseph's trip to Bethlehem might well be a Lucan creation. So, we ask, what is Luke trying to say here theologically? It's important to realize that Augustus is known as the Emperor of Peace; he created the *Pax Romana,* the Roman peace. He's associated with peace in the mind's of Luke's contemporaries, so Luke is going to present Jesus as the Prince of Peace born in the age of the Emperor of Peace.

Luke has the emperor calling a census for all of his people, because Luke has to find some way to get Jesus into Bethlehem. The reason is because the prophet Micah (5:1) seemed to say that the Messiah was going to be born in Bethlehem, David's ancestral city. Matthew had the same problem in writing his nativity story. He solved it by having Joseph already living in Bethlehem. But Luke has to get Jesus there from Nazareth. So he has the Emperor call a census, has Joseph's hometown Bethlehem, and then Jesus can be born there. More than likely, all these events are based on oral traditions in the Christian communities, on stories, legends, and a few facts all gathered together. I'm not denying Jesus might well have been born in Bethlehem, but that fact is not essential for knowledge of salvation.

In studying biblical writings, the evangelists are talking about salvation history, not about secular history. They are theologians, not journalists. In this light, certain things are simply not important. For example, to Paul — in complete contrast to Luke — Mary is not an important christological figure. In all Paul's writings, he never alludes to Mary and never alludes to the first thirty years of Jesus' life. Paul is fascinated with one thing — the living presence of Jesus in the church and in the creation of faith communities. Persons can live a full vibrant life in Christ without pondering questions like "How many animals were in the ark?" and "Was Jesus really born in Bethlehem?" Those aren't important questions. But because we are factual Americans and because images of Mary and mangers in Bethlehem are part of our mythological symbol system, we like to have the facts straight. We want to know whether or not an event really happened.

In Luke's version of the story, Mary and Joseph couldn't get into the inn, so she gave birth in a stable. These facts may be a personal reminiscence of Mary, and they may not be. Theologically, for Luke the inn that had no room for God might be a symbol of how God has not been received by the world. It certainly identifies Jesus and his family with the poor class.

"She wrapped him in swaddling clothes" (2:7). In the Hebrew Scriptures, both Samson and Samuel were wrapped in swaddling clothes. I always wondered what swaddling clothes were. I'll bet most people don't know. They're just bands of cloth, long strips of cloth. That's the way little babies were wrapped up, to protect them and keep them still. Mothers would wrap up the baby's body completely. I don't know what they did when they changed their diapers, but some say it was a form of diaper itself.

"The angel of the Lord appeared to them and the glory of the Lord shown round about them. They were terrified. but the angel said, 'Do not be afraid. Listen'" (2:8–10). We've always thought of shepherds in a sweet, romantic agrarian image of harmless little people. Actually, that's not the connotation of shepherds among the Jews. Theirs is a very negative one. Shepherds are people outside the system and outside the law ("sinners" in their objective way of thinking). They're associated with bandits, nonconformists, boorish and dirty folk. If Luke were writing his gospel for contemporary Americans, he might substitute for shepherds a group of rednecks, winos, or hillbillies. Luke wants to reprimand his readers, perhaps especially the rich and privileged ones, and chooses shepherds to make his point. He is telling them that it was the people of no regard, who were not part of the system, to whom the good news was first announced. These societal outcasts recognize what is happening, and they go running into Bethlehem to find this special child.

You might notice that we always put animals in our Christmas cribs, but there is no statement in Luke about any animals being near the manger. Our tradition goes back to the very first verse of the prophet Isaiah. "I reared sons. I brought them up but they have rebelled against me. The ox will know its owner, the ass will know its master, but Israel, you know nothing. My people understands nothing" (Isa. 1:2–3). So now we have the ox and the ass coming to the manger and, not only do they recognize their master, they discover in the manger the feed trough of life. Here in the manger is the Lord, who will feed the people of Israel.

"As for Mary, she treasured all these things and pondered them in her heart" (2:19). This is a phrase that Luke uses more than once to describe Mary's response (2:52). It has a tone of depth and excitement about it, and that's always the experience of the Holy: we're both fascinated with it and afraid of it. Luke shows us Mary caught up in this experience of the Holy. She is in that liminal space between fascination and attraction on the one side, and fear and awe on the other. When you confront the Holy, you stand between those two polarities, being pulled by both. All you can do is go deep and inside at the same time. God has overcome that transcendence and distance by becoming flesh in Jesus, who takes away our fear and satisfies our fascination about the invisible God.

Presentation in the Temple

During the presentation of Jesus in the temple, Luke introduces us to Anna the prophetess (2:36–38). In using the name Anna, he alludes to the scene in 1 Samuel where Hannah and Elkhanna brought Samuel into the temple at Shiloh and presented him to Eli the priest. To connect Jesus with this tradition, Luke has Joseph and Mary bringing Jesus into the temple and presenting him to Simeon the prophet. The connotations are similar. Just as Eli is excited at the birth of Samuel, so Simeon rejoices at the birth of Jesus and proclaims his destiny to Mary: *"You see this child, he is destined for the falling and rising of many in Israel, destined to be a sign that is rejected. And a sword will pierce your own soul too, so that the secret thoughts of many may be laid bare"* (2:34–35).

Many sermons have been based on that phrase, "and a sword will pierce your own soul too." Recall Christian art of the Mater Dolorosa, the Sorrowful Mother, with the sword through her heart; this verse is the source of that image. Simeon says to her, in effect, "Your heart is going to be cut open, but it's not just for your sake. If you can trust the pain and agony you're going to go through, you will become an instrument for many other people's hearts."

Many of us have to take that prophecy for ourselves. If the pain we're called to bear is not just for our conversion but for the conversion of many others, then we can perhaps bear it with joy, freedom, and even delight and trust in God.

But the sword may have other symbolic meanings. Luke is probably not trying to stress only the sword bringing sorrow, but the sword bringing definition and judgment. The sword, in Jewish imagery, is that which divides, that which defines and separates.

Later in his gospel, Luke will return to this theme. Jesus calls Mary his mother, but he says "physical motherhood is not where it's at" (see 8:19–21). Jesus was telling his mother that she had to let her son go, give up her physical motherhood of him, to create a larger spiritual family. Any mother would understand.

I know, for example, some of the mothers of our New Jerusalem Community members are sad when their children come to join our extended family. To their mothers, it feels like a rejection of their motherhood and the home they prepared. You can understand that disappointment. If you had a child and he or she went off to live in someone else's family, you'd feel, "Oh, my God, wasn't our home good enough?" It really hurts. We in America don't really understand the idea of a spiritual family, and maybe the Jews in Jesus' day didn't either, but Jesus was very much at work creating a new spiritual family out of the people of Israel.

Raymond Brown interprets the sword that pierces Mary's heart as the pain that Mary went through to give her son away to be the leader of a new people. She had to accept that he was no longer just her son, but he was the son of this new spiritual family. Jesus even went to the point of saying to her, "Who are my mother, my brothers and sisters? Whoever does the will of my Father, this is my new family. This is the family that lasts" (see Luke 8:19–21).

Jesus had to create a new spiritual family to break down national-ism and to break down the way blood families sometimes keep one another from God because of the tremendous social and peer pres-sure — and "blood" pressure — that can rise in families. Families often try to control one another. Parents can control their children for-ever by guilt and shame. Some parents are still controlling their "kids" who are fifty and sixty years old. The Lord had to free us from that kind of bondage. There's an important purpose to the natural family, but there can also be very destructive purposes.

As the infancy story ends, Luke has Jesus in the temple, representing Israel, his destiny being proclaimed both by the prophetess Anna and the prophet Simeon. The holy family fulfill the law and then they go back to Jerusalem (2:39).

Years in Nazareth

The Scripture scholars say that the story of the boy Jesus in the temple emerged from a famous saying of or about Jesus. The saying is, "Did you not know that I must be about my Father's business?" Perhaps he was already saying it as a boy.

Luke's literary challenge is to create a story around this saying. If you read the text carefully, you can see the unreality of some of it. Who of you would have a child and go an entire day on a journey and not notice your son was missing? Or not make sure he was in the caravan in the first place? If you take the story literally, Mary and Joseph don't look like good parents! But Luke isn't talking about how parents should or should not behave. He's creating a story building up to that punch line, and he's making it as dramatic as he can. The parents missed him. They can't find him among the caravan. They go rushing back to Jerusalem, asking everyone, "Where's our boy?" And there he is, standing in the temple telling his parents, *"I've got to do my Father's work"* (2:49).

After fifteen years of men's retreats, I can also add that this is an absolutely classic text for what must happen to a boy in his early teens: he must break with his mother's world and enter into the world of men. Not only does Jesus go through the needed initiation rites, but Mary allows it even though she does not understand (2:50).

Finally, at the end of chapter 2, Luke tell us, *"He went down with them to Nazareth and lived under their authority. His mother stored up all these things in her heart. And Jesus increased in wisdom and stature and in favor with God and society"* (2:51–52). There he lived, quietly, we assume, with Mary and Joseph for most of his life.

He must have received extraordinary love from them. We argue back to Mary and Joseph through Jesus. Any person who is as whole and free as Jesus was had to have extraordinary parents. They must have loved him without manipulation, without those primitive patterns of shaming and threatening that are so common. Our practical experience of the doctrine of original sin is in receiving and passing on, from generation to generation, *the lie that we are unlovable.* When we say that Mary was immaculately conceived (born without the effects of that lie) we mean, psychologically, that Mary was protected from the usual garbage from the beginning (which is, in turn, the creation of "saints" Anna and Joachim). Mary was protected from the lie. She knew she was good and belonged to God.

In German-speaking countries, there are often statues of St. Ann with the daughter and grandson in front or to the side of her. She is curiously called *Die Selbst Dritt,* or the Third Self. The people themselves wonder about this title, but now we know that their emotional intelligence was very insightful. Folk religion can be sometimes very destructive and sometimes pure genius. Mary, then, didn't pass on any garbage to Jesus, because she didn't have any!

If he had to be loved so perfectly by Mary, he would also have to be loved perfectly by Joseph; otherwise his young psyche would have been distorted. I don't know why we didn't transfer the freedom from original sin to Joseph too. It seems in this case to be a bias toward the feminine. I believe Joseph had to be an extraordinary man and father, or Jesus could not have so readily called God "Abba." He could never have so utterly trusted his heavenly Father and trusted the masculine word for God if he didn't have a human father who must have been very, very good. Luke wants us to see clearly and fully the humanity of Jesus. Yet he is preparing us for a revelation of his divinity in the next chapter.

Three

Jesus' Public Life in Galilee

Luke 3

I want you to understand that my observations on Luke's Gospel are selective. My point is not to share everything that may be scripturally important. My purpose is simply to teach you the way I work with the biblical text as a preacher. I hope the way I've been exploring Scripture in this book has already been freeing for you and teaching you how to approach the text yourself. The medium — my technique for approaching the Scriptures — is the message. Of course, this is not the only way to approach Scripture. The Spirit uses the sacred writings to reveal God in a variety of ways, perhaps in a unique way for each person and each believing community. But, however we approach the text, we must come with an attitude of faith.

In this book I know I sometimes slip into a preaching mode, but I'm primarily intending to teach. And teaching presumes faith. It doesn't really lead to faith, but *starts* with it. Much of our Catholic school system and religious education has bought into the false assumption that teaching leads to faith. It doesn't. The act of faith, the challenge of faith, the call to faith happens on an entirely different level from teaching. You can teach all you want, but if your students are merely operating in the realm of curiosity, it doesn't lead to a faith response.

At the same time, teaching lacks a certain power that I feel when preaching. When you dissect these different stories and approach them in terms of modern biblical criticism trying to understand what Luke wanted to say, you take away much of the power of the fundamental approach to preaching. Preachers, as a rule, don't bother discussing scholarly criticism from the pulpit. Good preaching simply takes the biblical story and communicates it in its concrete, immediate, personal categories. There's a special power in that kind of preaching. As soon as you begin to introduce ifs, ands, buts, or maybes into your homily, you qualify everything in the story, and that diminishes the power and focus in your preaching.

So we're doing something very special here. It's a kind of preparation for preaching. The reason I dissect the text is so I can understand it more deeply, and at several levels perhaps. But at the same time, when you go back as preachers — or however you use this gift — you can't speak from the pulpit this way. *You have to put the story all back together in a personal, concrete, immediate form and use it to communicate the Word of God.*

The point is that, if you've assimilated some of the best biblical scholarship, you are less likely to reach a dead end, especially in legalism and spirit-deadening literalism. Many destructive effects have been caused in the church because legalistic preachers have insisted that things had to be this way and no other. And even worse, much positive spiritual imagination has been lost by jumping to the dogmatic level or freezing the text with literalism. In other words, the effects of good biblical scholarship will most likely be evident in your preaching, not only in what you say, but also in what you don't say. The importance of keeping up with biblical scholarship is that we don't misuse the Scriptures and put people back under the law.

After we as preachers dissect the annunciation scene, for example, the important thing is not to speak to the people of scholarly debates about the meaning of the text. The important thing is to take Luke's concrete myth, story, and image in all its immediacy and personal appeal and *communicate the Christ message through that myth.* That's what Luke himself is doing, and we need to imitate his method in our time and culture.

The last line of chapter 2, *"Jesus grew in wisdom and grace,"* is a good takeoff verse to discuss the human consciousness of Jesus. It's hard for us to admit and accept, because of our Monophysite bent, that Jesus grew in knowledge and wisdom and did not possess all knowledge from the moment of his birth.

There are other verses, that suggest the same idea, for example, in the beginning of Romans: "Jesus Christ ... was proclaimed Son of God in all his power through his resurrection from the dead" (Rom.

1:4). Paul seems here to reflect an understanding that Jesus grew in knowledge of who he was. Neither Luke nor Paul intend to say that Jesus was not always the son of God. Jesus' objective divinity is an article of our faith. No one is denying that. John the Evangelist assures us of that at the beginning of his gospel. The preexistent Word, before incarnation, was always objectively the child of God. What Luke is telling us is that the *human* mind that Jesus possessed, functioning through his human brain cells, had to be fed with data and information just like yours and mine. That Jesus *grew*, humanly speaking, in body, mind, and soul, is the simplest way we can express that Jesus is both totally human and totally divine.

Helping Jesus come to know in his human mind *who he was* is the role of the Spirit in his life. (The Spirit has exactly the same role in each of our lives, of course.) We're going to see, in Jesus' baptismal scene, that the Spirit's role is to communicate to and convince the mind of Jesus who, in fact, he was.

For Jesus baptism is a great breakthrough point. As he is standing in the Jordan River, it becomes evident to him who he is when he hears the words, *"You are my son, the Beloved. My favor rests on you"* (3:22). Once Jesus grasps in his human mind that he is the son of God (to what degree, we do not know), he moves forward.

We know from our own experience that it is not enough to know interiorly who we are; we need confirmation of the fact from others. Identity is a social construct too. We ask others how they see us. Jesus does the same. For example, he asks Peter the disciple, *"Who do people say that I am?"* He asks, *"What am I for you?"* (see Luke 9:18–21).

The way we all come to know who we are happens, in great part, through other people telling us who we are. We learn elements of our identity in the ways they relate and react to us. And we never seem to stop inquiring about ourselves.

Throughout his life on this planet, Jesus' self-knowledge continues to grow. I don't know any contemporary biblical scholars who would dare to say, "It was at this point or that point in his life when Jesus fully realized who he was." Some suggest it was at his baptism. Others say his self-knowledge remained a continuously rising consciousness during his life. Others claim it was not until his resurrection itself that Jesus fully knew his identity and nature. Paul in Romans 1:3– 4 could be interpreted that way. Perhaps not until the resurrection did the human consciousness of Jesus come to understand what we would later call him in Nicene theology: the Son of God and the Second Person of the Blessed Trinity.

When you approach the gospels this way — with Jesus continuing to grow and develop in self-understanding — I think you'll find they'll become much more real and alive for you. The stories will become more identifiable and transferable to other persons and situations. Jesus will become a real model and mentor of the process of faith itself instead of just the object of our faith. We believe "in him, through him, and with him," as the Eucharistic Prayer says.

Luke tells us that Jesus walked the journey of faith just as you and I do. That's the compelling message of the various dramas where Jesus needed faith — during his temptation in the desert, during his debates with his adversaries, in the garden, and on the cross. We like to imagine that Jesus did not flinch, did not doubt, did not ever question his Father's love. The much greater message is that in his humanity he *did* flinch, *did* ask questions, *did* have doubts — and still remained faithful.

You see his faith tested in the temptation scenes in Luke 4:1–13. The question is constantly put before him: "Is your Father to be trusted?" That is the great question that the human race at the most basic level is asking: "Is God to be trusted?" If you examine your own experience, you can see we are constantly asking that question. "Is God to be trusted? Is the Father really *Love*? Is the Father also a nurturing Mother?" We hear Jesus continuing to ever more resoundingly answer, "Yes, God is on your side. Yes, God is more *for you* than you are for yourself."

John the Baptist

In chapter 3 Luke focuses again on John the Baptist. Luke gives him a great headline: "*In the fifteenth year of Tiberius Caesar's reign, when Pontius Pilate was governor of Judea...the Word of God came to John, the son of Zachary, in the wilderness*" (3:1–2). Some scholars suggest that, given the formality of the first verses of chapter 3, this was originally the beginning of Luke's Gospel. Their opinion is that the infancy narrative was inserted at a later date. These scholars are not saying that Luke's infancy narrative is incidental. Far from it. In fact, they say that the first two chapters of Luke are a summary of Christian theology. Some would go so far as to assert that every major theological theme developed in the body of Luke's Gospel has already been introduced in the infancy narrative.

We've heard these teachings of the Baptist read many times in Advent liturgies. What John represents is the earnest and heroic first stage of the God journey. It often seems to be the good and needed beginning. It's important to know that Jesus' gospel of love cannot be understood until we've first faced John the Baptist's gospel of repentance. It is the first step into the kingdom, and yet Jesus soon says, *"The least in the kingdom of God is greater than [John the Baptist]"* (Luke 7:29). An amazing paradox that has seldom been discussed.

Looking over the last twenty-five years of American culture, I think the reason why the hippie gospel of love was so hollow and did not bear fruit or last very long was because it lacked the necessary prior stage of repentance and conversion. When you preach love without conversion, you don't get lasting love. If you don't first call people to grow, to change, to call themselves into question, to be willing to go to a new level of consciousness, you can't sustain love for very long. In fact, you don't get genuine love at all. You get a temporary, make-believe, romantic, idealized experience, like the "love" young people often get caught up in: They wish to be in love and fantasize what it would be like to be in love. Or they repeat the love messages they hear in their songs: "Love is all you need." "Love is everything." "Love is the answer."

We can all agree with those slogans, but if you just preach them apart from conversion, change, and repentance, you are not preaching a credible or sustainable message.

As preachers, I think we've fallen short in that regard, not only in the more recent church, but even in the old church. In pre-Vatican II days, we were not expected to change and we were certainly not told that change would be the only constant in our Christian life. That's why Vatican II was so traumatic for so many of the clergy, religious, and laity. We were not taught the Baptist's gospel of change. We were not taught that life is essentially process and development and that healthy religion is always about transformation.

John the Baptist defines genuine repentance by its fruit — what we today call "results." "If you are repentant," the Baptist would say, "produce the appropriate fruits. Don't just talk about it, produce something new in your life. Make changes. Do not think of telling yourselves, 'We have Abraham for our Father' " (see 3:7–8).

If the Baptist were here in America today, he'd say, "Don't think of quoting your traditions, telling yourselves, 'We're Catholics, we're under the pope or bishop.' Don't hide behind authorities. Produce the appropriate results. Don't just stand on the past or hide inside some symbol system. I tell you, God can raise up Catholics out of these very stones."

The people asked him, "What must we do, then?" He gave them practical answers. *"If anyone has two tunics, share one with some-one who has none"* (3:11). How much more practical can you be? Theologically, Luke is saying, "If you really hear this gospel, you will recognize it as the gospel of a shared life. If those kind of practical acts of caring that John is mentioning aren't happening among you, I don't think you're listening to the Lord."

There were tax collectors who came for baptism, and these said, *"Master, what should we do?"* And he said, *"Exact no more than your rate"* (3:12–13). Specific and practical. Do you realize in America today how many well-intentioned Catholic businessmen think that following the Lord means simply going to church on Sunday — and not to cheat on their wives? Their business life is never called into question. The system they're supporting, day after day, is in fact, not paying a just wage, cheating the unsuspecting, and extorting unjust profits. The maximization of profit is accepted without question in America as a way of life, despite the Tenth Commandment.

Anthropologically, I am told, the world will be destroyed by greed and violence. Any truthful teacher or religion is going to put up bar-riers to both greed and violence. Jesus and John both put this truth at the center of their teaching, but it has consistently been ignored by Christians. Is there any other way to stop this cycle of greed control-ling our country? Addictive greed knows no satisfaction. Make more money, make higher wages. We always need more and more of that which doesn't work.

We can try all the available economic methods to change our ob-session with having more and more, but basically it's going to have to come back to the conversion of people's hearts from the way of greed. When everybody — business, management, and labor — wants more and more, someone has to say that greed is, in fact, opposed to the way of love — and that it is destroying the planet. There is a direct line from greed to a culture of violence, which is what we have now become.

In the preaching of John the Baptist we hear the beginnings of the call to create the new society. That's the social revolution Christianity should be bringing about. To avoid such a confrontation with society, we've spiritualized the gospel and what it calls for. We've said the gospel means to have a personal relationship to Jesus, which entails going to Mass on Sunday, singing spiritual songs, attending prayer meetings, reading the Bible, discussing theology. This approach simply does not question the lifestyle that follows from such belief. That kind of "spiritualized" gospel is dying, thank God, and deserves to die. And yet it's amazing how many people are still holding on to it.

John the Baptist is essential for a true understanding of the gospel because he does not allow the "spiritualizing" to happen. He says, *"Exact no more for your service than what you have a right to"* (3:13). Some soldiers asked him in turn, *"What about us?"* The Baptist, ever practical, said, *"Don't intimidate people. Don't manipulate them. No bribing, blackmailing, or extortion. Be content with your pay."* (see Luke 3:14).

Untransformed people will always be preoccupied with power — controlling other people, manipulating them, using them for our own gain. Sad to say, we understand relationships almost exclusively in terms of the pragmatic ways people are useful to us, which makes love and true community impossible. The gospel can free us from that.

"And so a feeling of expectancy had grown among the people who were beginning to think that John might be the Christ, so John declared before them all, 'I baptize you with water but there is one coming after me and he will baptize you in fire and the Holy Spirit.'
. . . There were many other things he said to exhort the people and to announce to them the good news" (3:15–18). Luke wants to make it very obvious that John the Baptist is only the beginning of the gospel, but he provides an essential beginning — of conversion, change, repentance, and very practical decisions.

John the Baptist is soon imprisoned (see 3:20). You don't talk that way in public without making enemies. You don't assert the social gospel as a prerequisite of the spiritual gospel and make many friends. If you preach a spiritual gospel, everybody likes you. They'll put you on prime time television because you're harmless. The comfortable members of the system will financially support you. Preach a pious gospel of "love Jesus and sing songs to Jesus" and they'll let you go. They won't take you seriously, but you're not much of a threat. If you begin to preach about the practical implications of the love of God and the freedom of God, as the Baptist did, they'll put you in prison (or stop donating to your television show) because you are starting to upset the system.

As soon as John is imprisoned, Luke immediately moves to the baptism of Jesus. If the authorities are going to lock up John and his gospel, Jesus is going to move forward in full force. But first, as we might say today, he has to put it all together.

The Mystery of Sonship

"After his own baptism, Jesus was at prayer" (3:21). Every chance Luke gets, he puts Jesus at prayer, because prayer makes things happen. Prayer opens us up to the presence and power of the Holy Spirit. Or if you resist religious language, we can say that prayer is simply the reconnecting of all things in the unity that they are.

"Heaven opened and the Holy Spirit descended on him in bodily shape, like a dove" (3:22). This is where we get the image of the Holy Spirit as a dove. Already in the church, even before Luke's time, the dove had become the primary Christian symbol or image of the Spirit. All four evangelists in recounting the story of Jesus being baptized use the same metaphor for the free and unrestrained gift of God. The Celts spoke of the Holy Spirit as the "Wild Goose." Some Christians take this dove symbol literally. A church in Europe claims to have a feather of the Holy Spirit in its relic box! That's what comes from a literalism that misses the real message in the image.

The revelation comes from the heavens directly to Jesus: *"You are my Son, my Beloved. My favor rests on you"* (3:22). The core of Jesus' message is tied up with the mystery of sonship and daughterhood. You have to understand this beloved relationship to understand the rest of the gospel. For Jesus, the mystery of divine sonship involves a relationship with God of dependency, intimacy, and trust; within this relationship, the revelation of the divine reality — who the Father is — is passed on to and received by the Son. As a result, whatever the Father is the Son becomes (see John chaps. 14–17).

For Jesus, "discipleship" is another word for sonship and daughterhood. Those who cannot be sons cannot be brothers and, finally, cannot be fathers. Those who cannot be daughters, cannot be sisters and, finally, cannot be mothers. Disciples must follow that sequence. This involves learning first how to be sons and daughters, learning how to be taught, how to receive love, how to be loved, how to be taken care of, how to be believed in.

But a proud and rebellious people do not like to be sons and daughters; they immediately want to be fathers and mothers, that is, they want power, they want to be in charge. Therefore, be careful of any fatherhood in the church that does not come out of primary sonship. And do not trust any fatherhood in the church that does not come out of practical brotherhood. It will have little true authority.

This is what religious orders were trying to do initially: provide settings in which we could learn to be sons and brothers, or daughters and sisters, before we attempted to be spiritual fathers and mothers. Calling each other "Brother" or "Sister," monks and nuns were supposed to have spiritual guides and directors and live under their care — learning how to be taught, how to receive love, how to be healed and transformed — before they would dare to father or mother others.

So Jesus, first of all, steps into his ministry as son, not as a father. Rather he lets the Father teach him. Because Jesus is always listening to the Father, the Father is continually teaching him, and his growth continues.

For example, you know that beautiful and powerful expression, "Amen, Amen" that was always used at the end of a prayer in Judaism? Jesus puts it at the beginning of everything important he says. Why would Jesus do that, since as a good Jew he knows the expression belongs at the end? What that probably means — at least the best I can come up with — is that Jesus is saying that he has already heard in his heart what the Father wants him to say. So when Jesus is saying "Amen, Amen," he is affirming what he has just heard interiorly from the Father. He then passes it on to us.

That means Jesus says nothing to us that he hasn't heard first. He teaches only what has been told to him, only what has been taught to him by the Father. He's, first, a faithful son; out of that sonship experience comes the power to be the father that creates this spiritual family, the church.

In his journey on this earth, of course, Jesus is quite comfortable being a brother. We're going to see how easily he moves among the people and lives as one of them, relating to them. He did not live in a clerical subculture like the ministry does today. He did not live apart. He lived with the people. He did not live separated from women. Luke is quite clear about that. In Jesus' entourage, Luke lists the Twelve and then indicates that a large number of women were moving around with Jesus (8:1–3). He's living a real-world lifestyle. That's what gives him authority to speak to that world with understanding.

All of you know what I'm talking about between the lines here. I think this question of a real-world lifestyle has to be dealt with in some way, if the clergy is going to regain its true fatherhood and learn how to speak again with authority to the world. The male club, clericalism, must go.

The Twelve were able to carry on ministry and not have to fish all day for their living because there were some kind women, apparently, taking care of them. Luke says these women provided for the group out of their own resources (8:3). So to be a brother and a son, you have to let yourself be loved. You have to know how to receive love.

After I left the exclusively male clerical world, where I had lived for thirteen years, and moved into the mixed households in the New Jerusalem Community, I first hesitated to let women love me. I always presumed something else was up their sleeve. We were taught to mistrust women, apparently as a way of protecting our "sacred selves." Unfortunately, there was little openness to allowing others to change us or even affect us.

To let a person love you and to allow yourself to love that person — that is considered a very threatening possibility in the priesthood. But Jesus allowed people to mother him and father him and allowed himself to be a brother to others. Out of that environment came his authority to be a wise and caring spiritual father himself.

What does Luke tell us about immediately after Jesus' baptism? Luke recites Jesus' entire genealogy.

If you compare Luke's listing of Jesus' ancestry to Matthew's, you find it's very different. Is someone incorrect, or are they coming from a different tradition? Neither. It shows they were not concerned about historical accuracy. Their concern is belongingness and sonship (The word "son" occurs over seventy-five times in Luke's presentation of the genealogy). They're saying, "He's one of this humanity that is ours."

The significant names in the listing, of course, would be son of David (v. 32), son of Abraham (v. 35), son of Adam (v. 38), and, finally, son of God (v. 38). This defines Jesus' sonship and says of whom he was son. When you know your grandmother prayed five Rosaries daily, suddenly that gives you your myth, your *Roots* experience. You know from whom you came. You know who you are.

In Jesus' baptism and his genealogy, Luke is defining the roots from which Jesus came. The Jesus story begins by telling us that Jesus was part of an eldering system of good, bad, and indifferent people — just like us. You don't have to have perfect parents to be on his journey.

Luke 4

Immediately after his baptism, immediately after Jesus is graced by the Holy Spirit, he undergoes the temptations. The same pairing of the baptism and the temptations is also found in Matthew's Gospel (Matt. 4:1–11) and in Mark's in a shorter form (Mark 1:12–13).

This sequence of events should come as no surprise. It is a classic and rather universal pattern of male initiation: trial, testing, facing and experiencing death, and coming out with a new identity and mission. Chapter 4 of Luke contains great theology in simple, story form.

Jesus' answers to the questions presented by the tempter are all taken from a section of Deuteronomy (see Deut. chaps. 6–8). In this section of the Hebrew Scriptures, God is summoning Israel to its destiny, and Israel is constantly tempted to disregard its destiny. Luke presents us with Jesus, the New Israel personified, being summoned by God to his destiny and experiencing the same three temptations, as the people itself did, to disregard and avoid their destiny. These three are the temptations that, in fact, apply to every age of the church in terms of ministry.

The Temptations

I see the first temptation, the one about turning stones into bread, as basically an invitation to doubt his vocation to sonship. This is what we all doubt. *"If you are the son of God..."* is repeated twice (4:4, 9) We doubt we are God's son or daughter. That temptation has to be dealt with at the beginning of ministry.

If I find I am working with people who do not know who they are, that foundational doubt must be cleared up first, or there is no foundation. In other words, they still need some major surgery. Until people know their identity in God, they're not going to have anything to say. Basic conversion is a reconstituted sense of one's own identity, a different sense of the "I" that I am — not me apart and alone, but me-in, me-with, and me-and Another.

Certain missionaries have succumbed to the first temptation. They give out bread instead of the word of God. They give out bread in an attempt to solve their own problems. Perhaps they feel guilty. Perhaps they have a need to feel effective. Perhaps they doubt that they have anything to give in Christ. Perhaps they don't know that they have anything to give in praying with a person and giving a person hope or love. It actually is far easier to give a person a five-dollar bill than it is to share your faith with that person. It actually is easier to feed a person a meal than it is to let that person see your life at a deeper level.

I'm not saying that we shouldn't feed people, or sometimes give a person a five-dollar bill. What I am saying is don't cop out with that. Don't avoid the immediate power of God's first liberation, the liberation of the self. Jesus is saying, "If you feed a man with bread, he will be hungry again tomorrow. He'll come back for more bread. And you'll get caught up in an endless system of feeding people bread instead of returning them to their radical dignity as beings-in-God. This is the power of who they are, so they can, in fact, make bread for themselves" (see 4:4).

It seems to me that Jesus' response truly respects the human being in a far deeper way. He operates as if we are already spiritual beings and our task is to live that in a human way. Most religionists seem to think we are merely human beings and we have got to try to become "spiritual." It ends up being a very different agenda.

Next, *"He showed him all the kingdoms of the world and said, 'I will give you all this power and the glory of these kingdoms'"* (4:5-8). It's interesting that here and in several other places in the gospel Satan is seen as the prince of this world. *"It has been committed to me and I give it to any one I choose"* (4:6). Sadly, that seems to be the truth of it. Jesus is Lord, but in a very real sense his Lordship seems to depend on our "yes." God so respects the freedom of men and women that God cannot come into this world except at our welcome and insistence.

Satan is, unfortunately, the prince of this world. Satan has the first chance at us because he doesn't respect our freedom. God respects our freedom, and will not come uninvited. Satan comes uninvited.

This second temptation is to doubt that the kingdom of God is here, because we are overwhelmed by the apparent kingdoms of business, money, the media, etc. We "worship" their influence and thus give

them even more. We're so overwhelmed by the sense of evil, so overwhelmed by the kingdom of this world, it is difficult to look beyond it and see the presence of God and the power of the Spirit. It is difficult to see, in the midst of the evil and darkness that seems to be overtaking the world, that God is still present.

Until and unless we can believe by the gift of the Spirit that God is winning — even now — we cannot begin. Jesus refuses to worship the false kingdoms and instead bows only before the hidden but real kingdom of God. It is a matter of seeing correctly and seeing the *transcendent within* of the entire material world. Without such seeing, there is no positive or hopeful foundation. Jesus sees that God *is* finally in charge and says, "Worship God alone" (4:8).

Finally, *"He led him up to Jerusalem and made him stand on the parapet of the temple. 'If you are the son of God, throw yourself down'"* (4:9–12). Here is summed up our doubt that God cares and that God can or will do anything. The only way many of us can believe is by signs and wonders. Jesus refuses to sell out to a gospel of signs and wonders. He refuses to entertain people in order to make them believe. If you believe only because you have seen a sign or a miracle, you do not really believe. The quick sense of awe and wonder you feel is not faith. It will soon fall by the wayside because it has taken no risks and plowed no new ground. Ironically, the only people for whom miracles are truly miracles are those who had faith before the miracle happened. They see in it a confirmation of the truth they already believe and praise God for it.

Two people can see a miracle. The one with faith will praise God, the one without will find some way to forget it or explain it away. That's simply been the history of Christianity. Miracles and signs don't produce people of deep faith, because invariably what such people want is another sign next Friday night to carry them through another week. That's the depth of their religion. God is more like their private magician than anyone they love and serve. Miracles are signs for those who *already* have faith — that God is in all things.

In this third temptation, Jesus refuses to sell out to the form of faith that depends on showy immediate actions of God. He says in effect, "Don't play games with God" (4:12). This temptation is the only example in Scripture of the devil quoting the Scriptures and, of course, for his own purposes. Surely a warning in itself of how religion can be misused.

"*Having exhausted all these ways of tempting him, the devil left him to return at the appointed time*" (4:13). The point that Luke seems to want to make here is that temptations never ceased in Jesus' life. He is a constantly tempted human, just as you and I are — to doubt, question, and wonder.

These three temptations can surely be seen as archetypal and universal patterns that all must face to be properly "initiated."

The Galilean Ministry

"*Jesus, with the power of the Spirit in him, returned to Galilee; and his reputation spread throughout the countryside; he taught in their synagogues and everyone praised him*" (4:14–15).

First we see them praising him. Next, he comes into the Nazareth synagogue and seems to have the role of lector. He stands up and picks out his reading. Immediately, he is going to tell them who he is. This is his "inaugural address," given at the beginning of his Galilean ministry. In effect, he tells them, using the words of Isaiah the prophet, "This is what I stand for." As soon as he connects the spiritual gospel with the social gospel, all of a sudden the people's praise turns to upset. Watch how it happens.

"*The Spirit of the Lord is upon me, he has been given to me, he has anointed me.*"

"That's a good beginning," they think. "That's good charismatic language." All the listeners are excited.

"*He has sent me to bring the good news to the poor.*"

"Oh, oh, where is he going with that?"

"*To proclaim liberty to those who are in prison.*"

"What does this mean? Is he against capital punishment?"

"*And to the blind new sight.*"

"Oh, well, we can spiritualize that easily enough. He's giving new faith to people without faith."

Why, of all the passages in the Hebrew prophets, did he pick this verse as his inaugural address? Isaiah 61:1–2 ends with a climax that would not have been lost on his audience: "*To set the downtrodden free, and to proclaim the Lord's year of favor.*" Ye gods! — the Jubilee Year, when all financial debts are forgiven!

I can recall groups I stood in front of in this country who felt quite sure they possessed the full gospel — we all want to think we do. I started preaching on themes of faith, trust, hope, Jesus, anointings, miracles, and freedom, and they were all cheering me on. As soon as I begin to talk about other topics — the Third World, shared life, commitment, poverty — I could see the facial expressions change all across the room. Then I could see the questions in their minds: "Is he with us? Is he one of us? I don't know if we like him."

When I stop halfway through my evening's presentation with the themes of hope and freedom, I get a great applause, usually a standing ovation. But after the second half, when I develop the social gospel, I usually just get polite applause. These are people who love to apply to themselves terms like "full gospel." But to them the full gospel is simply having a personal relationship with Jesus.

Such a personal relationship is great. I praise it. That's the power and source of the gospel and I'll never deny it. But that's only the beginning. If we don't carry through the initial relationship with Jesus and see the implications of it, this gospel is death — not life — for most of the world.

Realize that this full gospel has its vertical dimension (of us to God), just as it does the horizontal (of us to each other). Together they form the cross. The cross is the symbol of our faith. And we have to put both pieces of the symbol together. When we have the full gospel, vertical and horizontal, then the world can begin to believe that we're really a People, and we're not simply creating religions and feelings of righteousness for ourselves.

Jesus rolls up the scroll, gives it back to the assistant, and sits down. You can almost hear the uncomfortable silence in the room. *"And all eyes in the synagogue were fixed on him. Then he began to speak to them. 'This text is being fulfilled today, even as you listen'"* (4:20–21). He's saying, "That's what I stand for. That's my party platform." *"They were astonished by the gracious words that came from his lips. They said, 'But this is Joseph's son, surely?'"* (22–23). They're trying to apply some doubt to this situation, take away a few of his credentials. He conveyed an awful lot of authority and everybody at first applauded. If Jesus had been here among us today and read with the authority he displayed in Nazareth, we might have said, "Where did you get your theology degree?" "How do we know you're preaching the truth?"

"He replied, 'No doubt some of you will quote me the saying, "Physician, heal thyself"'" (4:23). "Some of you are saying inside, 'Don't you preach to us, you make sure you're doing it yourself.'"

"We have heard all that happened in Capernaum. Do the same here in your own countryside" (4:23). They're telling him, "Okay, if you're going to preach this hard message, we want to see you dance first. We're going to follow you, Jesus, only when we see the signs and wonders.

"And he went on, 'No prophet is ever accepted in his own country'" (4:24). He is unwelcome, so he leaves Nazareth, the town of his birth, and walks to Capernaum, another town in Galilee. He never *imposes* his truth by coercion or excommunication, as the church has often tried to do. He is willing to wait for depth, good will, and true faith.

In Capernaum, Jesus performs a few more signs. He cures a demoniac, he cures Peter's mother-in-law from a high fever, and he cures a number of people who came to Peter's home (4:31–41). He travels throughout Judea, healing another demoniac and doing several other cures.

"I must proclaim the good news of the kingdom of God to the other towns, too, because that is what I was sent to do" (4:43). This is Luke's first usage of "kingdom" language; with healing, all the elements of kingdom here-and-now are present. If our preaching never results in healing-transformation-regeneration, I doubt whether the preaching is true gospel. Jesus' ministry is always presented as a continual interplay of teaching and healing, the one following the other. Today many Christians are unexpectant of or even embarrassed by the prospect of healing in response to a sermon. How utterly strange and sad. Even we preachers would be surprised if our words were "effective."

Luke 5

In chapter 5, Luke relates the calling of the first disciples, yet Luke immediately defines discipleship in the story of Peter. Discipleship is defined in terms of risk and trust. *"Simon, put out into deep water and put your nets out for a catch"* (5:4).

Simon is the fisherman who should know the sea and understand it. At this point, there is no reason for him to trust Jesus, so he replies, *"We worked hard all night long and caught nothing. But if you say so, I will put out the net"* (5:5). So this new life, this new church, this new community is going to have to depend on people trusting the Lord and risking the Lord's truth even against their own temporary truth.

"And when they had done this, they had netted such a huge number of fish that their nets began to tear. So they signaled to their companions in the other boat to come and help them. When these came, they filled the two boats to sinking point" (5:6–7). He's preparing them to understand how they will gather the people of God together. It's a gospel of risk and trust that will call people together. Spiritual entrepreneurship, you might say.

"When Peter saw this, he fell to his knees and said, 'Leave me Lord, for I am a sinful man.' For he and all his companions were completely overcome at the catch they had made" (5:8–9). Somehow, these very practical fishermen saw, in this familiar realm of the sea, a sign of the transcendent. Here is an important point for preachers. We've got to find a way of letting people experience God at that everyday, workaday level, where, in fact, they're spending their eighteen waking hours.

Jesus knows how to speak to Peter in his fishing world so that it becomes a transcendent sign for him. In effect, Peter is saying to Jesus, "This is the world I know and I know how it works; if you can turn my fishing world upside down, you're for real." So Jesus isn't talking synagogue language or theological language, he's talking fishing language. That's the language he uses when he's working with Peter. That's the language and imagery best designed to lead Peter out of himself and confess his faith in Another.

"But Jesus said to Simon, 'Do not be afraid; for from now on it is human beings you will catch' " (5:10). This is only preparation for the real work I have for you, but the method will be the same: trust over calculation, love more than power, risk instead of security.

"Bringing their boats back to land, they left everything and they followed him" (5:11). Most scholars doubt that the departure happened *that* quickly, but the point is that the bonding — Peter's and Jesus' relationship — happened *that* quickly, like "falling" into love. Somehow, when Peter saw the power, freedom, and life that Jesus offered, he was ready to let go of everything he was sure of for what he was not yet sure of. It is Abraham's story repeated.

It hasn't changed, either. Abraham's story is in our world today, the world of our work. We tend to build our security, especially once we get beyond the age of thirty. Like Abraham, we're culturally defined by the pursuit of security. That's who we are. To question that pursuit in any way is threatening. To let go of their security is one of the greatest risks that can be asked of people. How difficult it is for people to leave their comfort zone or their self-image in order to go onto a new path.

After Jesus cures a leper (5:12–16), his reputation continues to grow, and large crowds gather to hear him and be healed. His preaching is constantly mixed with healing. We do need those holistic signs of being free — cures and healings — not only in our minds and spirits but in our bodies, memories, and emotions. That's the beauty of what we're coming to understand today about the full gospel. God has come to free us at every level of our being.

In the cure of the paralytic, we see that sin is not simply something we do; it is something we are. Sin is the distorted personalities people are trapped in. Sin is the illusionary lives that people live and the twisted motives that drive them. No one has ever taught them truth or meaning, so they live at a very low spiritual subsistence level. They are "paralyzed."

Sin is manifested in the oppressive and destructive lifestyles that totally wrap some people up, the unreal way some people have of relating. A family can easily get caught in that lifestyle sin. "Our family knows only one way to relate," a young person once told me. "We put one another down, we talk to one another negatively, our language is filled with sarcasm, resentment, and violence. It's the only way I've ever seen our family relate." Now if you grow up in a family environment like that, it's a most base and malicious kind of entrapment, because that's the only way you'll know how to relate for the rest of your life. That's sin. That's the sin that controls us and keeps us from living in the truth. It keeps us from seeing the vision of the whole. Sin is not just something we do, an isolated action. Those isolated actions or omissions are much more the *effects* of sin rather than sin itself.

The ministry of reconciliation and healing has been so superficial in the church because we have simply been dealing with symptoms and effects: "I did this three times and that four times." In our sacrament of reconciliation, there was no dealing with the heart, the person, no dealing with relationships — the places where sin lives. The realm of real sin has been kept in a private and disguised world. It is no surprise that so much of the gospel is about healing lepers and paralytics (5:17–26). That is how well evil hides itself — quiet slow paralysis and sins of social contagion.

Toward the end of the fifth chapter, Luke recounts the call of Levi, who is presumed by many to be the apostle and evangelist Matthew (see Matt. 9:10–12). In Jesus' day, a tax collector was a Jew who had sold out to the occupying Roman enemy, that is, he was hired by the Romans to collect taxes from the Jews for Rome. A tax collector was presumed to be an unfaithful Jew, one who not only let himself be bought out by the Romans but also was personally pocketing a good amount of the money he was collecting from his own people. The tax collector symbolized the Establishment with all its exploitation, extortion, cheating — everything people hated.

Despite this, Jesus called Levi to follow him as a disciple (5:27–28), and in response Levi held a great reception for Jesus in his house; the guests included a large number of tax gatherers. Jesus accepted Levi's invitation to eat with them (5:29). Jesus is not afraid to criticize the system, nor to confront it, but yet he knows the people within the system, like Levi and his fellow tax collectors, are still human. As we say, he is able to distinguish between systems that trap people and the individual person.

Jesus teaches by his life and not just by his words. He teaches, as the Hebrew prophets did, in what are called symbolic prophetic actions. Jesus is aware that symbols, actions and images speak much more powerfully than words. For him to sit at table with tax collectors is a powerful symbolic action that confronts the hypocritical religious system of the Jews. It says in effect, "You condemn the corrupt Roman political system, but you maintain a corrupt religious system of your own."

Table fellowship seems to be the central symbolic action of Jesus. He is invariably eating with the wrong people, at the wrong place, saying the wrong thing and eating the wrong food — always to redefine and reimage the social order and human relationships. In Luke's Gospel alone there are ten such examples! As a teacher of God, Jesus' action was meant specifically to say something about who God is and those whom God would call friends. When Jesus sat down to eat with these "tax collectors and sinners," it made the Jewish officials who heard about the dinner ask themselves the question, "Could we have been wrong about God? If Jesus is doing this, what does he know about God that we don't know?" (see 5:30).

When he said, *"It is not those who are well who need the doctor but the sick. I have not come to call the virtuous but the sinners to repentance"* (5:31–32), the Pharisees and their scribes knew he was saying something new about the nature of God. In contrast, we seem to be saying, "We have the perfect medicine — just make sure *you* are so perfect that you will never really need it!" Jesus knows that until we *need* mercy and forgiveness, we will never know who God is — or who we are. That's revolutionary.

Luke is developing important theology here. To do it, he continues to use eating language. The Pharisees and their scribes complained to Jesus: *"John's disciples were always fasting and saying prayers, but yours go on eating and drinking"* (5:33). The Jewish officials were trying to accuse Jesus of being a libertine or a liberal — someone who was doing his own thing and not strictly following the law of Moses.

Jesus' reply was, *"No one tears a piece from a new cloak to put it on an old cloak. If he does, not only will he have torn the new one, but the piece taken from the new one will not match the old. No one puts new wine into old skins. If he does, the new wine will burst the skins and run out and the skins will be lost. No. New wine must be put into fresh skins* (5:36–38). Using the image of the wineskins, Jesus says that the medium must also be the message, the structures must not just talk about "grace" but must themselves be grace.

In effect, Jesus says: "Yes, I'm a friend of John. Yes, I'm building on John. But can you really hear what I'm saying? You're going to have to let go of John's system in order to understand me. My message is about new wine and new wineskins. My good news is not just rehabilitating or patching up John's message."

Jesus was calling people to a whole new way of acting and organizing — not just new words. We must *see* the implications of this "new wine" through new wineskins. New ideas demand new groups and structures that *model* the new way of thinking practically — or we really don't get it! This has always been the unheard message of Jesus. Instead, we still use words like "celebration" to describe dead ceremonies; we speak of the Spirit through structures obsessed with management and control; we talk about community and justice using images of patriarchy and injustice. It will never work because no one believes it — or sees it. Then both message and medium are dismissed as irrelevant.

Luke 6

"The human person is higher than the Sabbath law" (Luke 6:5). Had moral theologians of earlier centuries taken more seriously this passage about the disciples picking corn on the Sabbath (6:1–5), they would have seen that Jesus was very clearly saying the law is not an end in itself.

When I was learning about healing ministry from Francis MacNutt, he told me that in spiritual healing one of the most difficult demons to exorcise is the demon of legalism — the false belief that God and the law enjoy the same authority, and that to obey the law will bring salvation. Whoever before thought of legalism as a demon that needed to be exorcised? MacNutt had made an important discovery.

Clergy and religious of the past decades were so trained in the saving power of the law that some had come to believe that observing the law was tantamount to holiness. Once, when preaching a priests' retreat, a priest stood up and defended this position — without blushing. I replied, "Father, I simply can't support unquestioning obedience to the law. That's absolutely opposed to the gospel. The law does not save or necessarily lead to love, God, or truth. That should be obvious to everybody by now." I don't think he agreed with me, but the point must be made clearly or it will always be avoided, especially by those in religious "management" positions. I have found that if you tamper with people's punishment/control system, you frighten them at a very deep level. I guess many think that religion is for the sake of social control. This does not seem to be true for Jesus at all.

Jesus went out of his way to remind the Pharisees and his disciples that David, the perfect Jew, did what was against the Hebrew law by eating the sacred bread on the holy table. Jesus said, in effect, "You all know the Pharisees would get very upset if someone tried to do that today. Well, David did it" (6:4). We can imagine their attempts to reply: "There was a reason," or "Well, that was way they did things back then."

In other words, Jesus was saying, "You have to realize that people were not made for the law, the law was made to benefit people." As he put it to the scribes and Pharisees, *"Is it against the law on the Sabbath to do good, or to do evil; to save life, or to destroy it?"* (6:9) The fully alive human being is the end and purpose of the law. God did not come to earth to provide us with a police force. God came to set people free to live and live more abundantly. Whenever we find ourselves valuing laws before people, we had better put ourselves under the judgment of the gospel once again. The gospel is about divine union and all the dead-ends it takes to get there. It is not a system for control of the masses. If it is, it has had little success.

The challenge is to preach a gospel that is livable, believable, and life-giving. Perhaps that is the most simple criterion by which we can discern the teaching of the Lord. It is always a call to death but it is always life-giving in the long run. When you see life being created between people and within people, you see the Spirit of God. Where you see the Spirit, you will always see freedom (see 2 Cor. 3:17).

We Catholics have not been a people characterized by freedom, nor have we appreciated freedom. The church should have been in the vanguard of freedom, but it wasn't. Now the freedom promised us by the gospel has been distorted into license, rebellion, and willfulness. We failed to model the synthesis and made the antithesis inevitable.

For the most part, our morality has reflected culture and been afraid of the true freedom of the gospel. It is to our eternal shame that we can't say it was the church that raised our consciousness about slavery, war, racism, just wages, totalitarianism, or sexism. Instead it was the movement of God in history that did it; the church merely came running along behind and said, "Yeah, that's right, that's right."

Why are we not a people who have been freed by the gospel? Why are we not first to step forward and lead the world in seeing the freedom that God has offered us? The answer is, we're afraid. We've been under the law and held down by the law for so long, that we're no longer a creative and imaginative people listening to the next word of the Lord. We're busy trying to get "saved." As another Gospel puts it, John (love) gets to the tomb and believes first; Peter (church) "follows" and does not understand (John 20:4–10).

Let me sum it up in this way. Eternal life is not something that is sought after. Eternal life is something that is responded to. That means it's a gift. We don't have to fight for it. We don't have to work hard to earn it. We don't have to obey laws in order to deserve it. We already have it. Love knows that.

Jesus' State of the Union Address

If "the Spirit of the Lord is upon me" in chapter 4 was Jesus' Inaugural Address, the last half of chapter 6 was his State of the Union. He tries to describe what it is like to live the happy life, the freed life, the united life, the life that is in touch.

In his talk he's not presenting a list of actions that you must do in order to get into the kingdom; he's describing for the disciples what it means to already be a disciple (6:20). Matthew has Jesus giving this talk to a huge crowd (Sermon on the Mount, Matt. 5–7), but Luke says it's given only to the disciples, because for him it is precisely a description of discipleship. It is much more direct and even confrontational than Matthew's "eight beatitudes," even if it is descriptive.

In fact, Jesus was saying, "If you are a disciple and you have been transformed, these beatitudes are going to make sense to you. However, if these beatitudes don't make sense to you, then you still have a way to go. You haven't yet experienced eternal life." Read Jesus' discourse that way. See if his "four beatitudes" make sense to you or not. If they seem nonsensical, ridiculous, absurd, paradoxical, and you cannot understand the God language here, then perhaps you have not yet experienced eternal life.

"How happy are you who are poor, yours is the kingdom of God" (6:20). Right now, if you can be free to be economically poor, to be psychologically disarmed, emotionally vulnerable, spiritually naked, socially without reputation — without all those things that protect you, give you power, and exalt you — you *are* in the kingdom.

"Happy are you who are hungry now, you shall be satisfied. Happy are you who weep now, you shall laugh" (6:21). There is an almost Zen-like quality to these statements: riddles given by the master to make us redefine our reality. He praises what we would normally avoid — hunger and mourning — so that we need a new life paradigm to understand what he is saying. Remember that no problem can be solved from the same consciousness that created it. The spiritual teacher is always trying to destabilize our old consciousness, in this case, where satisfaction and laughter are the goals, and replace it with an utterly different worldview based on radically different assumptions and goals — a new universe of meaning!

There is no other way to understand the final beatitude than to submit to a "great reversal." *"Blessed are you when people hate you, and when they exclude and insult you, and denounce your name as evil on account of the Son of Man. Rejoice and leap for joy on that day! Behold, your reward will be great in heaven. For their ancestors treated the prophets in the same way"* (6:22–23). When we realize this does not describe us (surely not all of us!), we know we are not yet living from within the true paradigm of eternal life, which is very liberating for the true self and unmasking of the false self.

There are four beatitudes in Luke, but eight in Matthew (Matt. 5:1–12). Luke fills out the number with four maledictions that continue to subvert our false universe. *"Alas for you who are rich. You are having your consolation now. Alas for you who have your fill now. You shall go hungry. Alas for you who laugh now, you shall mourn and weep. Alas for you when people speak well of you, this is the way your ancestors treated the false prophets"* (6:24–26).

Don't make laws out of each of these beatitudes and maledictions by saying, "I now have to go out and do the right things." Here, as always, Luke is trying to create for us the myth of the kingdom, presenting it in imagery that he knew would shock us and force us to go deeper. He wanted us to ask ourselves: "If this passage is true, then what is God all about? What endures in life? What's the really real? What is eternal life?" Truly meditating on these four questions — and the four beatitudes — frees us from selling out to the present age and enables us to see the vision of the whole.

When St. Thérèse, the Little Flower, was caught up in her little embarrassing and painful moments of the day and her emotions were taking over, she was not free to be present to that moment because she was hurting so much. She explained, "At times like that, what I do is try to get God's perspective. I figure God sees everything — the beginning, middle and end of my life. I imagine he's sitting up on a cloud, looking down on the whole of my life, so I try to crawl up on that cloud. Once I get up there and look down on my whole life, I don't take this moment too seriously. Then I don't get trapped by it."

You see the irony? The freedom to *live in* the present requires that you be *free from* the present. To truly give yourself to right now, today, you have to embrace the vision of your whole lifetime — time and eternity. Crawl up on Thérèse's cloud! That's what Luke's Gospel is trying to help you do in such a passage: It gives you the vision of the whole so you're not trapped, enslaved, and controlled by the present moment. On the other side, when you know that everything is important, then no-thing really matters and you can let go. *The* big story frees you from the tyranny of me and now. Your identity is from God and you enjoy the divine perspective. One person's lack of recognition of you or criticism of you is not going to destroy you — because you are named by God. That is the religious reference point that simultaneously grounds you and frees you. It is the only way out of the revolving hall of mirrors.

The Mystery of Forgiveness

Jesus continued his State of the Union: *"I say to you who are listening: Love your enemies. Do good to those who hate you. Bless those who curse you. Pray for those who treat you badly"* (6:27–28). Absurd teaching! Impossible teaching! Unless you have responded to eternal life. Then you understand the teaching; it makes sense and you can give yourself to it.

I want to use this passage to talk a little about the mystery of forgiveness. Forgiveness of our enemies to which the gospel calls us can be understood in a way that's better than we're used to. If we think of forgiveness as big-heartedly forgiving or forgetting other people's faults, this is not really forgiveness but rather an act of mercy and condescension on our part. Big-hearted me.

Most apologies people make to you are sort of embarrassing and don't work out, because in granting them you look like you are big-hearted, magnanimous, a great person — and very often the other person is demeaned. It doesn't really make others feel better about themselves; they just feel you are big-hearted. Of course, we would appreciate having some big-hearted people around us, but Jesus is asking us to go one step deeper in understanding forgiveness.

Jesus is not saying, "I'm big hearted and you're sinful." When Jesus forgives, it's not so much an act of mercy as it is *an act of loyalty to the truth*. Forgiveness is loyalty to the truth of who you are. To truly forgive someone is to recognize who they are, to admit and affirm who they are, and to know that their best selves will be brought out only in the presence of an accepting and believing person. *Forgiveness is basically the act of believing in another person and not allowing that person to be destroyed by self-hatred.* Forgiveness involves helping people uncover their self-worth, which is usually crusted over by their own self-hatred.

This is a way of forgiving people that does not make you look good *but makes them look good.* That's the way God forgives us. In the act of forgiveness, God gives us back our dignity and self-worth. God is loyal to the truth that we are. God affirms that we are good persons who have sinned. God asserts we are not bad.

By forgiving one another in this way, telling one another that we are good people, we allow ourselves to keep our self-esteem and dignity, to believe in ourselves. That's the way God treats us. That's why forgiveness is better understood not as an act of mercy and condescension and big-heartedness — although it includes that — but is much more an act of being loyal and faithful to a person and believing in that person. That's the nature of God's forgiveness.

If you don't understand that sense of forgiveness, reflect upon it and recall your own experience of forgiveness and apology. Remember that forgiveness is not just you fulfilling your obligation to be a forgiving person; the important thing is the healing and transformative effect it has on the other person.

You can turn forgiveness into an obligation, saying: "The law requires that I forgive everybody, so to be a good Christian, I'll forgive this person. That will fulfill my obligation. Now I'm a good Christian because I've done what I'm supposed to do." In behaving this way you have not necessarily really loved that person. Since forgiveness is a type of loving, the important thing is the *loving* of that person and the re-creation of that person, not necessarily our fulfilling our duty to be forgiving.

Jesus goes on with this theme: *"If you love those who love you, what thanks can you expect? Even sinners love those who love them. If you do good to those who do good to you, what thanks can you expect? If you lend to those from whom you hope to receive, what thanks can you expect? Even sinners lend to sinners. Instead, love your enemies and do good to them"* (6:32–35). So give to others what is God's. Do unto others as God has done unto you. God gives of the divine self generously and does not ask if we are able to give back. This commandment is utterly impossible to obey (or even understand) unless we have been transplanted into a new identity and a new world order. It forces us toward a new consciousness, where we *must* rely upon God to do it through us. We *know* that we can't.

"Be compassionate as your Father is compassionate" (6:36). It is not just the *imitatio Dei*, but presumes the *experience* of God's compassion and the life of *union* with that "energy." In other words, don't read this as a motivational pep rally, you-can-do-it-if-you-try-harder kind of talk, but much more a call to an "identity transplant," an ut-

ter transformation of consciousness that allows me to read reality in a new way. Some of Jesus' teaching has been rediscovered in the modern age by psychologists and therapists. Now we use words like "projection," "denial of the shadow," and "scapegoating." But Jesus had already told us about these things in prepsychological, image-based language.

"*Why do you observe the splinter in your brother's eye and never notice the plank in your own? How can you say to your brother, 'Let me take out the splinter that is in your eye?'*" (6:41–42) Much of Jesus' teaching for creating this New People has to do with healing, reconciliation, and forgiveness. Those themes will never grow old and never retire in importance. In fact, they might be more important than ever as our access to history increases.

It is difficult to present the core gospel message in many areas of the world where the "gospel" has already been preached. I realized this when I went to the West Indies. I almost wish I could be a missionary in some portion of West Africa that never claimed to be Christian so I could preach the uninterpreted, simple gospel of Jesus Christ. But when I go into South America or any place that claims to have heard the gospel, I have to spend 90 percent of my time undoing the past and explaining why former Christians didn't believe the gospel or live it.

If I went to South America — or anywhere, for that matter — on a permanent basis, I think my ministry would have to be largely healing, reconciliation, and forgiveness. When that realization hit me, I went back to the gospel and recognized that was precisely what Jesus was doing. He was in a culture where he couldn't move forward with the good news until people could let go of the past. History just keeps repeating the cycle of violence until someone gives us a way out. The gospel allows the new to happen. The gospel of forgiveness tells us to let go of all hope for a better *past*.

Once when I was talking with a group of young black men in the Virgin Islands, they said, "We want to be Christians, but when we go back to our friends, all they say is that it was the Catholic Church that justified slavery. Jesuit priests kept slaves."

I said, "I don't know my history well enough. Maybe that was true. But can't you let go of it? We only have one life. Right now. We can always find a justification for our anger."

The One replied, "Father, we're willing to let go of it, but our culture keeps reminding us of it. Everybody says, 'Why are you going to be a Catholic? Why a Christian? Those religions don't free us. They have oppressed us.' "

I want to just sigh with pain for God's people. How can anyone move us forward? How can anyone free us when we constantly hold on to hurts? And especially when most of the hurts really happened? History has become a giant glacial freeze of remembered hurts and justified retaliation. Nothing truly "new" is going to happen in history without the mystery of forgiveness. Greed has become resentment, and the cultivated resentments have become glorified violence in every century and every culture. "Who will deliver us from this body of death?" asks Paul (Rom. 7:24). Only the gospel.

Jesus can't create a New People without reconciliation and healing. Finally, he said to them, *"Why do you call me 'Lord' and not do what I say?"* (6:46). The doing is now urgent.

Luke 7

The cure of the centurion's servant is interesting because the centurion is not a Jew. He is a Roman, or at least a gentile. Luke has Jesus speaking this line at the end of the story, *"Not even in Israel have I found a faith like this"* (7:9). That would be like me telling nonbelievers in a Christian country that *they* have it together. Jesus' inclusiveness is really quite extraordinary. He seldom validates the tidy religious identities and boundaries that religious people would hope for. He would not please many contemporary conservatives.

The disciples of John the Baptist came up to Jesus and said, *"Are you the one who is to come, or should we wait for someone else?"* (7:19). Jesus refused, as always, to get into any kind of theological debate. He simply said to look at what was happening and read the signs of the times. *"Go back and tell John what you have seen and heard"* (7:22). The blind see, the lame walk, the lepers are cleansed. Again, he's saying, in effect, that he fulfilled the prophecy of Isaiah. *"The lame walk, the lepers are cleansed and the deaf hear. The dead are raised to life and the good news is proclaimed to the poor. And happy the man who does not lose faith in me"* [sometimes translated as "not scandalized in what I am doing"] (7:22–23).

It's interesting that Luke puts that final line in there about not losing faith in Jesus. He almost seems afraid that people are going to want theological satisfaction more than a God at work in the world healing people. He has Jesus say, in effect, "I hope this doesn't scandalize you, but this is what I am doing. I'm not building buildings, I'm not teaching songs. I'm out on the streets healing people, liberating them, and telling them about life and love and what matters."

He has just healed a pagan's servant and raised a widow's son to life (7:11–17) without any question of orthodoxy, attendance at synagogue, morality (there are some very good arguments for the centurion and his servant being a sexual relationship, which is why he doesn't want Jesus to enter his house), or even future requirements to follow the law! He just sees pain, need, and a vulnerable, trustful human request — and he acts! No wonder he himself ends with a line to the effect, "I hope the church is not scandalized in that" (7:23).

But of course, the church is scandalized by anyone who heals and liberates people, still to this day. We are convinced that church is about gathering in buildings, singing songs, annulments, and attendance. Do you realize what a historically distorted development of Christianity that is?

Now our church is almost totally controlled by its real estate and bureaucratic procedures. Clergy and religious are obliged to staff offices and manage real estate as a major part of their work — not that such work is wrong or always inappropriate, but it's a matter of emphasis and importance. A Benedictine priest said to me once, "We started the abbey to run the school and now the school runs the abbey." I can just see all the religious nodding their heads. They know it's true. We are not free to ask, "What is the need now on this earth? What does God want us to do?"

Priests in Europe tell me how most of their time is spent as museum curators and fundraisers to maintain buildings built from the tenth to the nineteenth centuries. We've got our white elephants sitting in every city in the nation absorbing the bodies, minds, and spirits of the clergy. In one building, we Franciscans moved down from the third floor and then to the second, and now we're all on the first floor. I joined a committee for the Franciscans — which is unusual, since they usually keep me off committees — assigned to study the possible closing of some of our major institutions. It took the energy crisis to make us face up to the fact that we're not living poverty any more. One of our big buildings was costing $350 per day to heat! (That was, I grant, in January and February). How can we justify maintaining that building any more? Especially with only five people wandering around the first floor — and homeless people nearby on the streets!

How simple, pure, and straightforward Jesus' gospel is. He's dealing the issues of the heart and teaching the way of transformation — to help people remain alive, in love, and in touch. I'm not so sure the majority of our ministries are dealing with the growth and transformation of people any more. The main ministries supported in our church today are administration and teaching, so much so that 80 percent of our resources go toward offices and schools. Where's the ministry to the refugee? To the divorced? Why are they not equally important in building up the church? Where is ministry to the homosexual? Where is ministry to all the people that nobody is taking time to understand? Why does the ministry of healing and social outreach not look like real ministry to many priests? Is it because we have found our identity largely through administering sacraments (where we are in charge), as opposed to issues of transformation, where we can never say we are finished or "in charge"?

John's messengers went back. Still, the people were scandalized, so Jesus explained himself again in another comparison: *"John the Baptist comes not eating bread and not drinking wine and you say he is possessed. Now the Son of Man comes eating and drinking and you say, 'Look, a glutton, a drunkard, a friend of tax collectors and sinners'"* (7:33–34). No matter what we do, Jesus seems to say, you complain. *"We played the pipes for you and you wouldn't dance, we sang dirges and you wouldn't cry"* (7:32). Whatever is being presented to you, you find a reason to complain about.

I find that any reaching out to a *chosen* state of resentment is, ironically, used to deepen the resentment. When people have decided that they have a right to their negativity or it becomes their "niche," they will actually fight you if you offer them a way out.

I have lived in the old pre-Vatican II church, gone through the transition, and lived thirty years in the new church, and it has been interesting to watch the patterns. Many laity and religious who found reasons to not cooperate in the old church found another set of reasons in the new to maintain their uncooperative stance. Thanks to Vatican II, we've freed ourselves from all that old legalism, and the same complainers say, "Ah, things aren't like they used to be, you know. I'm not going to do this new stuff; this isn't like the Old Church."

I say, "Listen, you didn't do the Old Church either." I must sound pretty arrogant saying these things. I wouldn't have the nerve to say them, except it is the import of this Lucan text. It's what Jesus is saying to his contemporaries. He's saying, "Don't complain about what I'm teaching, because you didn't do the old thing either. You didn't listen to John, and now you're not listening to me. I can't take you seriously at all."

Jesus is not afraid to call a spade a spade. Sometimes we've attributed to him a very soft definition of love, but love, for Jesus, is intrinsically tied up with truth. He's not afraid to speak truth, which always cuts our human hearts open.

In the next beautiful passage — Luke's enacted parable — we have the woman who was a sinner(7:36–50). Jesus mixing with a woman of bad reputation and allowing her to touch him and wipe his feet is forcing his Jewish contemporaries to ask themselves, "Could we possibly have been wrong about God? If the way this man Jesus is relating to her is right, good, and from God, then maybe we don't know God." Realize that Luke here is not addressing his gospel to the Pharisees, who would probably never bother to read what he wrote, but rather to the people in his community, some of whom still have a tiny and tidy notion of God.

If you're lovingly in touch with the Spirit, you'll be like a movie screen. And your screen, as when theater screens grew from regular size to cinemascope size, will always be expanding. Always. When you find your screen contracting, i.e., your perspective on life in this world and in the Lord is narrowing, you'd better ask yourself if you're still open to the Spirit. Because your screen is designed to keep expanding and stretching. When your screen grows enough to cover 360 degrees, you've got the vision of the whole. That's heaven! Starting with a tiny screen, we finally need to get to circle vision, where there is room for sinful women, diversity, intimacy, and scandalizing of the comfortable at the Lord's table. Note the upset of the host and guests at Jesus' behavior: *"Who is this man who thinks he can forgive sins?"* (7:49). We would rather keep her in her sins and ourselves in our moral certitude than allow someone to widen our screen.

Luke 8

In the beginning of chapter 8, Luke tells about the women accompanying Jesus and the Twelve: Mary surnamed Magdalen, Joanna the wife of Herod's steward, Suzanna, and several others who provided for them out of their own resources. It's an extended family of those *"who had been cured of evil spirits and infirmities"* (8:2). Jesus was creating a new relational system that didn't fit any familiar mold, and it was scandalous to many. One even wonders how the contemporary "family values" camp would respond to Jesus. He is not modeling the modern nuclear family.

At this point, Luke begins a section full of parables. Notice how myths and parables interact. Our *myth* is a symbol system out of which we think and operate. Everyone has a myth. We have to have our myth because it creates our world and provides our frame of reference. In contrast, a *parable* confronts our world and subverts it. It doesn't call for discussion, debate, or question; it is not God-as-information. Rather it is God-as-invitation-and-challenge. A parable calls us to insight and decision. A parable doesn't lead us to endless analysis; it's either a flashing insight or it's nothing. Like a joke, it leads up to the punch line. Either you get it or you don't. You know how embarrassing it is when everyone is laughing and you don't "get" the joke. We should probably suffer the same embarrassment when we don't "get" the parable.

Jesus uses parables to give us images of the kingdom. His first one is the parable of the sower, which in Luke has been allegorized. An *allegory* is a literary form in which every line symbolizes something specific. This interpretation is given quite specifically in verses 11–15, so it is no longer an open-ended parable.

You who have been in ministry know the power of this allegory. You keep putting out the seed — the Word — and it is always received on various levels depending on where people are. Apparently, Jesus had the same experience and warns us against expecting a uniform or predetermined response. (Personally, this was the passage that gave me the permission to make my first set of audiotapes in 1973.)

After the allegory of the sower comes the parable of the lamp. *"No one lights a lamp to put it under a bowl or under a bed. He puts it on a lamp stand so people can see the light when they come. Nothing is hidden but that it will be made clear. Nothing secret but it will be brought to light. So take care, now, how you hear"* (8:16–17). The gospel is a call to live in the light. Many believe that Jesus told us to be good. But using the image of this parable, the Lord has not so much called us to be good but to be honest, to live in the truth, and in that way to be good.

Even the Greeks realized the greatest wisdom was to know yourself. St. Teresa of Avila called it the first and necessary Room of the "Interior Castle." The Lord's gospel frees us to live in the truth about ourselves. Only those capable of living in the truth are really capable of being good, in the true meaning of goodness. Nice action without truth is not goodness. Too often I agree with people's action, but their energy and motivation is all wrong — which finally spoils the correct behavior.

If you repress, deny, or pretend, I promise you the truth is going to come out in disguised form. It always will. In one way or another, you must face the shadow side of yourself. If you don't face the shadow within, you create enemies without. You project the enemy out there.

After all his years studying human nature, Carl Jung would say we basically project outside ourselves what is happening inside. We hate and attack it over there instead of in here. People who are always seeing enemies out there, those who are trying to "get them," will only continue the futile spiral of violence — and nothing new ever happens. If we are not "light" and "unhiddenness" (v. 16), we will invariably be blaming, accusing, and attacking.

I am trying to connect Jesus' universally true message with contemporary psychological language because it is the only way we think today. We are a psychological people. You can say, "But that's humanism, that's dangerous. It's un-Christian!" I say there is no other way an American born in the twentieth century can think except subjectively, personally, and psychologically. Jesus is making the same points except he's using mythological language and images, like seeds and lamps, which his audience knew how to understand. Jesus is talking "psychology," if you will. Remember, there is only one truth. Psychology and theology are both working toward that same truth, and we have nothing to be afraid of in any of the arts and sciences if they rightly describe the universal patterns. We need them all.

"His brothers and mother came looking for him, but they could not get near to him because of the crowd. He was told, 'Your brothers and mother are standing outside and want to see you.' But he said in

answer, 'My mother and my brothers are those who hear the Word of God and put it into practice'" (8:19–21). Those who *do* the truth are my family. Luke is telling us that Jesus has created a totally new definition of family that transcends blood lines and marriage. It is easy to belong to the right group, but much harder to belong to God. Much of religion is preoccupied with group identity more than falling into the hands of the living God.

Luke tells the following stories in this chapter to show that Jesus is about setting everything free. First comes the calming of the storm (8:22–25). The Jesus who can free our hearts to live in the truth can free all of nature to live in peace, because he controls even the winds and the sea.

In the story of the Gerasene demoniac (8:26–39), Jesus has power over evil and he sets the demons free. This is also a fine analysis of cultural sin and how we hold one another "in the tombs" (v. 27), nor do we welcome any change in the arrangement. I have treated this passage in more detail in my book *Simplicity,* chapter 6 (Crossroad, 1992). In the cure of the woman with the hemorrhage (8:43–48), we have a surprisingly revelatory story of Jesus doing what medicine is unable to do. In the raising of the daughter of Jairus (8:40–42, 49–56), he displays his power over death and sets the child free to live again. In the next chapter, he gives these powers to his disciples, the power to transform nature, evil, the body, the soul and even death.

Luke 9

"Jesus called the Twelve together and gave them authority over all devils and to cure diseases, and he sent them out to proclaim the kingdom and to heal" (9:1–3). First, he gives them advice for the journey. Road tips. *"Take nothing."* Be simple and open. Don't put your trust in possessions. Take *"neither staff nor sack nor bread nor money. None of you take a spare tunic. Whatever house you enter, stay there"* (9:3–4). The important point seems to be, "You remain mobile and free to go to them." Don't set up a world where the people you serve must come to you. He even calls the Twelve to be dependent and needy so they go as receivers and not just the guys with all the answers — a very vulnerable and never very popular notion of ministry. Francis of Assisi was one of the few who took it seriously.

Again, don't try to make a set of rules or laws out of this advice.

Luke is presenting an image because he knows images are what move us. This is the image of the free lifestyle, the mystical adventurer who has put his trust in God and not in the things of this world. He says, in effect, "Your lifestyle is what will give you the authority to preach to the world."

"Whatever home you enter, stay there. When you leave, let it be from there. As for those who do not welcome you, when you leave the town, shake the dust from your feet. So they set out and went from village to village proclaiming the good news and healing every-where" (9:4–6). It's hard to believe that this little ragtag collection of men following those simple instructions could possibly have been the beginning of what we call the church, especially when you realize the worldwide, complex, hierarchical, institutionalized structure the church has become. Does that mean that we're completely wrong? I don't think so, but I do think it means we have to get back to a much simpler, more vulnerable gospel. The gospel we are familiar with has become so acculturated, so interpreted and so filled with barnacles and encrustations that it will not be easy, especially in places where it has been around the longest.

I think it would be safe to say that Jesus has a different agenda. He's working toward something other than what many of us are working toward. His mission is something very simple and basic, but powerful, and we must rediscover these essentials.

"On their return, the apostles gave him an account of all that had happened. Then he took them with him and withdrew to a town called Bethsaida where they could be by themselves" (9:10). Notice this cyclic movement that occurs again and again in Luke: First, Jesus is by himself, then he is with only the disciples, finally they move into the crowd.

This is how Jesus teaches them. It's his seminary, his lifestyle, the way he does it. He takes them with him and, watching him, they learn the cycle and the rhythm of his life. He doesn't teach them merely con-ceptual information as we were taught in our seminary. He introduces them to a lifestyle. The only way he can do that is to invite them to live with him.

"But the crowds got to know where he had gone and they went after him. He made them welcome and he talked to them about the kingdom of God and he cured those who were in need of healing" (9:11). Can't you just see the apostles standing at Jesus' side, watch-

ing him, noticing how he does things: how he talks to people, how he waits, how he listens, how he's patient, how he depends upon his Father, how he takes time for prayer, how he doesn't respond cynically or bitterly but trustfully and yet truthfully.

"*It was late afternoon when the Twelve came to him and said, 'Send the people away and they can go to the villages and farms round about so they can get lodging and food. We are in a lonely place'*" (9:12). How does Jesus respond to this proposal? "*Give them something to eat yourselves*" (9:13). Luke is giving us an image of Jesus' ministry lifestyle. In effect, Jesus says, "You've been fed and taken care of by me, now you feed the others."

"*We have no more than five loaves and two fish . . . for there were about five thousand men, and he said, 'Get them to sit down in parties of fifty'*" (9:14). Among other things, this is a teaching about building community. You've got to divide crowds up. Get them into small groups. No way are these big groups going to become communities. Twelve is about the upper limit for a group where people can share life. After that it gets impersonal, legalistic, and ritualistic. Jesus could manage to keep twelve together in a community. For the rest of us, between six and nine persons is much better.

Jesus instructed the disciples to break them up into small groups. "*They did so and made them all sit down. Then he took the five loaves and the two fish, he broke them and handed them to his disciples*" (9:15–16). He said, in effect, "Now you distribute them to the crowd. You make disciples, who will make disciples, who will make disciples." The "cell" concept of committed believers was unfortunately taken more seriously by communism than by Christianity.

"*They all ate as much as they wanted; when the scraps were collected they filled twelve baskets*" (9:17). The final image seems to be one of fullness, satisfaction, plenty — a cornucopia of food — with leftovers for the outsiders. It might also be a reference to the early "bread and fish" tradition (the agape meals, pot-luck suppers for all that Paul talks about in 1 Cor. 11:17ff.). Unfortunately, the bread and fish meals seem to have died out in favor of the more ritualistic bread and wine tradition. Cultic religion won out over social religion.

"*Now one day when he was praying alone in the presence of his disciples*" (9:18) — he put this question to them: "'*Who do the crowds say that I am?*' *They answered, 'John the Baptist. Elijah. Or one of the prophets come back to life.*' '*But you, who do you say that I*

am?' It was Peter who spoke up. 'You are the Christ of God' " (9:18–
20). Basically, Luke is saying that Peter is the spokesman for this little
contingent of faith; he is their mouthpiece.

Luke is telling his people that the Twelve themselves do not realize
the full import of who Jesus is at this point. In fairness to the gospels,
there's no way that Peter's profession of faith at this time implied a
complete knowledge of Jesus as "Second Person of the Trinity." That
would be ridiculous. People like to put impossible affirmations in the
mouths of the apostles. All Peter knew at this point was that Jesus was
special to God. "Christ" means the anointed one, but it does not mean
divinity. For us "Christ" has come to mean divine sonship because we
have subsequently identified him as such.

"He gave them strict orders not to tell anyone about this" (9:21).
The crowds are going to have to find out for themselves. Jesus says, in
effect, "If they want to find out who I am, they themselves are going to
have to walk the same faith-journey you are on. If people say I am the
Christ just because it is a church dogma or because it is the cultural
thing to do, they don't really believe it."

Unfortunately, this is in fact where many of our contemporary
Christians are at. They affirm Christ's power and divinity because it is
family tradition or doctrine, but not because they have come to know
it experientially. Recall the beautiful line of David DePlessie, "God
has no grandchildren. God has only sons and daughters." Every generation has to be transformed anew. All we can do is invite, model and
share our experience of Jesus.

Right after Peter's affirmation of faith, Jesus predicts his passion
and names the conditions for following him (9:22–24). Realize where
this gospel is going to take us, he tells them. It's going to lead us to
lose everything.

It's like the girl in the New Jerusalem community who told her
boyfriend last week, "Listen, you better know how needy I am. You
better put on your track shoes now and run away from me before we
fall any more in love. If you marry me, you're going to have a hard
life."

I couldn't believe her honesty. She said to her friend, "I need a man
so badly, but I'm giving you your track shoes. Run now."

He said, "I'm staying."

She said, "Okay."

What that young woman did is exactly what Jesus is doing here.

He's saying, "I know you're falling in love with me, but you better know where this is going to lead you. I'm giving you your track shoes right now. You can run, but if you keep falling in love with me, it's going to lead you to death. It's going to lead you to lose everything that you think is important to you and that your system says is important. Do you want to stay?" They said yes, it seems, and that became the first generation of the church.

Overviewing the entire middle section of the gospel, it is clear, to biblical scholars at least, that Luke is gathering and adapting material from three or four different traditions — maybe more. He selects the material from these sources that he finds helpful to make his points to the community for which he is writing.

We often mistakenly think that Luke and the other evangelists wrote their gospels as if they knew we would be reading them millennia later. Can you imagine any contemporary author writing a book for an audience in the year 4000? Not likely for Luke either. Like any author, Luke was thinking of his audience and their needs here and now. He wanted to help them to live better lives and to answer the troubling questions that were bothering them.

As far as we can tell, in this section Luke was probably writing a manual for missionaries going out from his community. The text was designed for the training, enlightenment, and psychological support of missionaries. These new disciples of Christ needed to understand themselves — their identity, goals, and problems — before they went out. That seemed to be the organizing principle by which Luke chose this material.

Transcendence and Immanence

In chapter 9 Luke recounts the transfiguration (9:28–36). I'm sure you're familiar with the text. The account is also found in Matthew 17:1–9 and Mark 9:2–10, but with some differences. It has been conjectured by some scholars that the transfiguration scene is a misplaced resurrection scene. That may be right, because in light of the rest of the gospels, where we see a very human Jesus, we wonder how this transfiguration scene got put right in the middle of the story and where it came from. The three evangelists seemed to use it to support the divinity and transcendence of Christ. They are telling us that the all-too-human Jesus has another side, expressed in a mystical union with his Father.

This event reveals Luke's ideas on transcendence and immanence. Only in this single scene does Luke present the transcendent Jesus, while throughout the rest of the public life, Luke emphasizes the immanent Jesus. Consider immanence and transcendence as two ends of a spectrum. Looking at the sweep of Christian history, the church has always placed an emphasis on one end or the other. But 90 percent of the time, the emphasis has been on transcendence, the divinity of Christ, the utter otherness of the Lord.

The Christian history pattern is ironic, because the synoptic gospels stress his immanence, incarnation, closeness, and humanity. Yet the whole New Testament — all the Christian Scriptures together — maintains a beautiful balance between the two. God is totally beyond us, yet in Jesus God is also among us and within us — a creative tension that needs to be maintained both in experience and in theology.

If we wanted, in our time, to recreate a healthy gospel, truly an experience of the holy, we would have to find that synthesis — Jesus totally divine and totally human. You may think this synthesis is just a conceptual theological doctrine, saying, "Well, we have that doctrine straight in our head; he's totally divine and totally human." But that doctrinal balance has many practical implications. The way we believe that doctrine affects our whole behavioral style as Christians: our understanding of liturgy, morality, spirituality, and lifestyle.

As I said, the greater part of the Christian tradition, anxious to prove the divinity of Christ, has stressed his transcendence. "He is divine; he is God." It is what some have called the "pedestalization" of Jesus, putting him up on a pedestal so much that he is apart from us — sometimes "worshiping" him so we don't have to imitate him (a clever ruse!).

We see a pull in the other direction in the Franciscan movement, with Francis's strong appreciation of the humanity of Jesus, the person of Jesus, the closeness of Jesus to us. Recently, a strong move toward his immanence also occurred in the Charismatic movement. Though the Charismatics certainly believe Jesus is Lord, how is it that in a church they feel free to talk, mix, hug, relate, and laugh? That's a big difference in behavior. Thirty years ago, to talk in a Catholic church was tantamount to disrespect for God.

Because different theologies were at work, we have been pulled, in a very short time, from the transcendence to the immanence side. I think that shift is good for us. It provides an appreciation of the incarnation, the acceptance of the Spirit within, the recognition of the brotherhood of Jesus. Nowadays, when the good news is announced and received, we revel in the immanence and closeness of God.

According to Rudolf Otto's book *The Experience of the Holy,* the experience of the Holy lies between those two extremes. The transcendent God calls us to be awe-filled: to be fascinated by God's greatness, beyondness, beauty. God is beyond, totally beyond. God is wholly other. At the other end of the spectrum is the sense of God as one among us; God is attractive, compassionate, and with you — someone to whom you want to draw close. God fascinates and draws us out of ourselves.

To fully experience the Holy is to stand between those two extremes. It's like being pulled by two magnets. We're unbelievably attracted to be close to God, yet we pull back in reverential fear before the awesome divine presence. That's a hard balance to find. But that would seem to be the balance of the gospels and the balance we see at the transfiguration scene.

On the one hand, Jesus is shining with the glory of the Lord. Notice that the glory is coming directly out from him (v. 29); it is different from the glory of Moses, who shone because he looked upon the face of God and reflected God's glory as a mirror would. In the transfiguration scene, Jesus is not merely a mirror of God. Luke has Jesus shining of himself, thus identifying him with Yahweh. As bright as the Sun, "as brilliant as lightning." And yet Peter is so attracted that he wants to put up tents to preserve the wondrous experience (v. 33).

A good contemporary image of the Holy occurs in the last thirty minutes of the movie *Close Encounters of the Third Kind.* Remember the giant space ship hovering over Wyoming. It's an awesome experience. Totally other. Otherness always causes us fear. We're comfortable with that which is around us. Anything which is alien, anything "other" that we don't understand, always arouses fear in us. In the film we see these identifiable middle-class American people looking up at the space ship — the totally other, the beyond. They're waiting, as it descends, to see if it is a malevolent or a benevolent presence. Good or bad. The transcendent is always perceived as exclusively one or the other.

Horror movies present the transcendent as a bad presence. That's usually the expectation we have of the Other — that it is going to be evil. Yet the beautiful surprise — and the experience of the last minutes of *Close Encounters*, as the space ship opens and the figures emerge, who are totally other — is that they are full of light. The peace that comes from them is full of benevolence and kindness. The light that shines out from the space ship draws everybody toward it. In fact, the "Everyman" figure, a middle-class American man, is a good symbol of a true disciple, risking everything — his marriage, his family, his house, his money — to follow this star, this spaceship. In a moment of foolhardiness, stupidity, absurdity, and yet ultimately common sense, the man runs into the space ship. He risks everything he is sure of for what he does not know.

As an exercise, we could list the virtues that characterize one theology and the other. Virtues that accompany a transcendent theology include: responsibility, obedience, justice, discipline, long-suffering, self-denial, patience, humility. These virtues are well exemplified in our old liturgy — the genuflections, the bows, the incense, the altar rail with God on one side and us on the other, fasting from midnight, women forbidden in the sanctuary. The pre-Vatican II church provided a total mythological system to preserve and emphasize the transcendence of God. At communion time, we approached the Holy on our knees at the communion rail. Somehow our tongues were more sacred than our fingers. So we received the Lord only on the tongue. In many ways it worked to preserve the mystery side of God and religion.

The immanence virtues, however, are also a part of the biblical tradition. When we emphasize that God is among us, that Jesus is our loving Brother, that God is an incarnate presence in our midst, we emphasize the following virtues: personal growth (holiness is wholeness), spontaneity, freedom, love, understanding and being understood, sensitivity, fulfillment, authenticity, confrontation. With an emphasis on immanence, God is happening right here, right now.

Too much transcendence encourages a sin-focused spirituality, where the emphasis is on the many ways we can offend God. Every time we turn around, we can commit a sin because we're so unworthy and God is so great. In contrast, people overbalanced on the immanence side almost forget sin. Emphasizing God's immanence, we're so sure of the love of God, of the presence and acceptance of God, that we tend to forget the reality of sin, the possibility of us hardening our hearts and saying no, or being nonresponsive to love and simply closing ourselves up.

Even "love" has a different meaning in each approach. Transcendence spirituality understands love as the love of restraint, of discipline, of withholding, of respect, of sacrifice. In our immanence-centered age, we have almost totally gone to the other spirituality: to the love of expression, the love of union, of celebration. Celibacy, for example, which was revered in transcendental spirituality, is less appreciated today, because in immanence spirituality the only way to love someone is to express it and experience it now.

The experience of the Holy is found somewhere in the middle — between the immanent God and the transcendent God. That's what we want to find.

Power Struggles

Toward the end of chapter 9, Luke relates the disciples' argument along the road about who is the greatest among them (9:46–48). It is placed as a dramatic counterpoint to the previous verse where he predicts the low road of suffering for himself (9:44). It is no doubt an already experienced pattern, that church leaders are seeking position and power — while wearing pectoral *crosses*. He is telling them, "If you're caught up in power struggles, if you're all trying to be better than the other, you do not understand Jesus."

Men are trained to be competitive from childhood at home and in school. Catholic high schools train boys to be physically competitive. Seminaries train us to be intellectually competitive. The business world trains men to be economically competitive. Today, women seem to have picked up many of these same traits in the name of liberation. We cannot doubt that competition is totally ingrained in us. We bring competitiveness and other addictions to the building up of the church, and the believing community is no longer an alternative society.

Jesus now makes use of an audiovisual aid to break the disciples' addiction to power: *"Jesus knew what thoughts were going through their mind, and he took a little child and set him by his side. He said, 'Anyone who welcomes this little child welcomes me. Any one who welcomes me welcomes the one who sent me. For the least among you all, that is one who is great'"* (9:47–48).

In defining discipleship for these missionaries, Luke is continuously turning their worldly system upside down. He says that to give up the need to be in power you have to be as "useless" and vulnerable as a child. A child, by definition, is out of the system of adult comparison. A child in Hebrew society was not an innocent or sentimental image, but much more one outside the world of production, usefulness, power, and competition. Children were "nothing" that mattered. It is much more an image we would now associate with desert fathers, Zen masters, or St. John of the Cross. It is the language of emptiness, and we have largely missed its point by making it sweet. Children are quite simply *not adults* — and all that adulthood pulls us into. Maybe we forget that Jesus was also a "desert father" and used their radical images.

But the disciples are slow learners. Listen to their next line: *"Master, we saw a man casting out devils in your name, and we tried to prevent him because he does not follow in our company"* (9:49). Read: "Because he's not a Catholic like us, he's Assembly of God, we tried to stop him."

But Jesus said, *"You must not stop him. Anyone who is not against you is for you"* (9:50). He says, in effect, "Don't take it upon yourselves to judge people, or to divide religious groups into all wrong or all right. Don't create problems that aren't there." It's usually more a control issue than it is love of God or love of truth. Whenever Jesus' own followers try to turn his message of nondomination into domination, Jesus turns against his own! Quite amazing, really. As you know, we in our churches haven't learned that lesson too well. We still spend much time fighting one another and putting one another down, saying, "I'm right and you're wrong."

It's ironic that this very line "Anyone who is not against you is for you" is completely reversed in another place in Luke's Gospel where it says, *"Anyone who is not for you is against you"* (11:23). Maybe Jesus made both statements, but they are certainly saying different things. Which one are you going to use?

It depends on what situation you are in. That's exactly why the use of the Scriptures takes wisdom, intelligence, discernment, and honesty. This shows how free the early Christians were to understand the gospels. They were not, for the most part, using them dogmatically as we do. We tend to use the words of the text as an absolute law that applies in every case. Words simply don't have that efficacy and absolute quality about them. You can't take a certain phrase from the Scriptures and say that it is going to apply in every situation.

We misuse Scriptures by taking lines, absolutizing them, and making dogmas out of them. I call doing this "creating a paper pope": to take a line from Scripture and make an infallible statement out of it. For example, this tactic is common among people who use Scripture texts apart from their contexts. You can't do that with honesty or intelligence. The context is the environment in which we know the truth. Truth belongs to an entire situation, not to any individual line. *"Anyone who is not against you is for you"* applies in the context of people doing good, such as healing and casting out devils (9:49–50); but when you are forced to make a choice between good and evil, there is no room for compromise, and the statement *"He who is not with me is against me"* applies (11:14–23).

Text outside of context is almost always a distortion, and sometimes a real disaster. Now perhaps we would say "intellectual intelligence outside of 'emotional intelligence' is, finally, not intelligence at all." It usually misses the real point.

The Galilean ministry section ends with this poignant warning against group-think — *"Anyone who is not against you is for you"* (9:50) — before Jesus heads toward Jerusalem and the larger world. A gem of a transition. He makes paranoid, defensive thinking well nigh impossible. He takes from his true disciples the possibility of all scapegoating, turf battles, and group competition. What hope he offered history!

Four

The Middle Section
of Luke's Gospel

Luke 9 and 10

Jesus now sets his face to Jerusalem. He begins this new section with another warning about the misuse of power by his disciples. The Holy City is a spiritual symbol in Luke's Gospel; it is a very important symbol to him. The first scene in Luke's Gospel occurs in Jerusalem, the last scene is just outside Jerusalem. It is the city of Jesus' destiny. He is always oriented toward Jerusalem. Why?

I remind you, Luke is not a Jew, he is not writing for Jews, and yet he has totally accepted the Jewish myth and symbol system because Jerusalem is the symbolic center of God's action. Jerusalem is the microcosm of what God is doing on earth. It is all of history written small — or large — depending on your perspective. You can probably make the same statement today. People are excited to go to Israel, and yet saddened at the rivalry and hatred between the races, the denominations, and the churches in the city of Jerusalem. Many say it is a very unpleasant place to visit because there is so much hatred, bigotry, and prejudice in that city. The stones seem to hold a kind of negative energy in the very place we call the Holy Land! Saddest of all, much of it is happening among Christian denominations.

Maybe you have heard how some of the great churches have been sectioned off: Roman Catholics can conduct worship only in this section, Orthodox in this, and Protestants of these denominations can stand only in this section. On Easter Sunday, for example, if you attempt to cross over your denomination's line, you might be physically restrained.

In that sense, Jerusalem is still a microcosm of the world — a symbol of what we humans haven't yet learned. Ironically, in Jerusalem is also the hope of what we could learn. The light is still in that city. It is still the center of three great religions of the world: Judaism, Christianity, and Islam. All were founded or somehow associated with the city of Jerusalem. The greater a light you are, the greater a shadow you cast. When there is positive spiritual energy, there always seems to be negative too.

The Lord has given Jerusalem as a spiritual center to the world. The Holy City is enlightening and hope-filled, as Isaiah described it, "Above you Yahweh now rises and above you his glory appears. The nations come to your light and kings to your dawning brightness" (Isa. 60:2–3). And yet the same city seems to spawn the terrible evil and ugliness of sin. Jerusalem sums up the human situation. Like the Bible itself, Jerusalem is a "text in travail."

Such is the case for Luke. *"Now as the time drew near for him to be taken up, he resolutely took the road for Jerusalem and sent messengers ahead of him. These set out and they went into a Samaritan village to make preparations for him"* (9:51–52).

Maybe this "sending messengers ahead of him" could be spoken of, in our terms today, as preevangelization. However, the first experience of Jesus' messengers on this new missionary journey is rejection (9:53). You can almost see the missionaries coming back to Luke's community saying, "Gosh, we were trained here for two years but when we got out there, it didn't work." Don't think all missionary endeavors in those early days worked well, that strangers were overwhelmed with the presence of the Spirit, or that every thing the missionaries attempted succeeded.

"But the people would not receive him because he was making for Jerusalem. Seeing this, the disciples James and John said, 'Lord, do you want us to call down fire from heaven and burn them up?'" (9:53–54).

They're intoxicated with their authority and their influence. And when you are self-absorbed, you treat all rejections as *their* problem: "These secular and materialistic Americans are just hardened to my spiritual message," " . . . to the authority of the pope" — or whatever! You want to call down fire from heaven on *them,* instead of admitting that you might also be the problem.

For years, God has been warning me about this ego-inflation. It sneaks up on you slowly. I got used to big crowds following me, I got used to standing ovations, I got used to everybody asking me to sign their Bibles. Pointing to their Bible, I'd say, "I didn't write that," and get a big laugh, but I'd autograph their Bible just the same.

"Wow," they'd say, "you're quite a teacher and preacher and everybody likes you and listens to you." After a while, I got used to that adulation and approval. I thought everybody was going to like whatever I had to say. The truth was that, when I stood up in front of a crowd, I would make sure to say things people would like.

One day, I was getting ready to speak to a big crowd, a familiar group; I knew what would really turn them on. Just before I went up to the podium, God spoke to my heart: "Now, Richard, do you want them to love you, or do you want them to love me? Or do you want them to get to love themselves?" That was probably the beginning of a more honest and prophetic preaching on my part, at least I hope so. But such demons do not depart after one encounter.

I often speak in California at the Anaheim Convention Center. It is a fantastic feeling of power to stand up there with a little microphone and talk to a huge arena filled with thousands. People all around, including cardinals, bishops, priests — and even the apostolic delegate one time — all focused on me. It was intoxicating to have the feeling that I could control this crowd for an hour. It's actually very helpful to have some people come up afterward and tell you that you made no sense. Not much fun, but surely good for my soul.

Maybe this example puts it on a big scale, but in every one of our lives, the question will still be the same. The same power needs can be at work in controlling two or three people in your living-room prayer group.

God has to call us out of our need to control, to change, to convert other people. We are not called to control, change, and convert other people, we're simply called *to be present to them* and *to be Jesus to them*: to be present to them as he would be present to them. He takes it from there.

If he wants to convert, control, or challenge them, then that's the Spirit's work. Our job is, as was his in his earthly life, to come into the world, to be present, and to speak a word that is truth and life-giving. Then it is all up to God.

"So Jesus turned and rebuked them and they went off to another village" (9:56). Again, when they try to use his message to their own

ego/power needs, Jesus turns against his own and redirects their path. Brilliant! Others are not always the problem. Maybe *you* are.

As he heads toward Jerusalem, he is symbolically accosted by three people with three problems that usually keep us from the spiritual path. Note that all three are worthy responsibilities that we would all take as common sense: (1) the necessity of home and place, (2) "sacred" duties, e.g., burial of one's parents, and (3) relationships with family. Let's look at each of them.

1. *"As they traveled along, they met a man on the road who said to them, 'I will follow you wherever you go.' Jesus answered, 'Foxes have holes and the birds of the air have nests, but the son of man has nowhere to lay his head'"* (9:57–58). This is, again, the Jesus of the little ones, Jesus outside the system of producing and consuming, Jesus the poor, "homeless" one. There is apparently something more important than house and home, real estate and domestic tranquillity.

2. *"Another to whom he said, 'Follow me,' replied, 'Let me go and bury my father, first.' But he answered, 'Leave the dead to bury their dead; your duty is to go and spread the news of the kingdom of God'"* (9:59–60). Burying one's dead is a very understandable duty. And Jesus makes a very hard point here. The fact that Luke brings up this issue shows he's telling his community and his missionaries that the call of the kingdom is absolute. It's the only thing that matters, it's the only thing that lasts against all odds and obstructions.

So Luke is willing to question even the burying of a father, and he has Jesus say, *"Leave the dead to bury their dead"* (9:60). He's saying, in effect, "Forget about any other primary values you may have had. It's going to take this kind of urgency to *get* the point and to get refocused on *one* transcendent reference point. Both are monumental transformations of consciousness."

Jesus obviously isn't telling people simply not to go to a family funeral; there might well be a wisdom way to do both. You can go to a parent's funeral but with a transformed consciousness as to its meaning. You will then be a lightning rod for the transformation of others. I have attended just such "larger than death" funerals.

All in all, Luke's trying to point out how hard it is to be faithful to the Word. (I wonder what literalists do with this passage, by the way.)

3. Finally, *"I will follow you, sir, but first let me go and say good-bye to my people at home"* (9:61). As before, he's saying this to a people to whom the family was a primary value. They had much

tighter family units than we do in America today. Why would any
human being disagree with: *"Let me go and say good-bye to my
people at home."* Yet *"Jesus said to him, 'Once the hand is laid on
the plow, no one who looks back is fit for the kingdom of God' "*
(9:61–62).

Family, marriage, and children are commonly used as avoidances
and excuses for not walking a spiritual path. Jesus says, "Don't turn
back. Don't waver. You must keep moving ahead." That's how you
come to know yourself, by a "long obedience in the same direction,"
holding fast to your faith, and listening for the next word of God. But
that certainly doesn't mean you don't visit your mom and dad once in
a while. Again, an honest reading of the text is at the same time much
harder and much easier than a mere literal or fundamentalist reading.

Luke 10: Mission of the Seventy-Two Disciples

"After this, the Lord appointed seventy-two others" (10:1). Where
does the number 72 come from? From Genesis 10 some say that there
are seventy-two nations on the earth. So what Luke in his universal
gospel is saying is that Jesus' word is meant for everybody on the
earth, so he gives Jesus seventy-two disciples.

*"After this the Lord appointed seventy-two others and sent them
out ahead of him in pairs to all the towns and places he himself was
to visit"* (10:1). Somehow, by their love, their life, their words, the
seventy-two have to prepare the hearts of the people to understand
what Jesus is going to say. Maybe they're primarily witnesses, in other
words, people who live a believable life, a real life, an attractive life.
When people see us living a believable life, they are ready for the *how*,
the *why*, and the deeper message.

For many years we sent out New Jerusalem Community teams.
Sometimes I was invited to a place where I was not known. If the
community teams visited there first, or if the people had heard of the
brothers and sisters of New Jerusalem, I came in with full authority. I
can understand, therefore, what Jesus experienced, because the teams
were my letters of recommendation. After strangers saw the community teams as believable people, who were real, loving, and spirit-filled,
it gave me an authority I would otherwise not have had. That seems
to be what Jesus is doing here.

"He sent them in pairs ahead of him" (10:1). Luke has a theology
of twosomes. As far as he is concerned, the gospel of love cannot be

communicated by one person because, in the end, love is something happening between two. Jesus knew that too, of course. If only one disciple is sent, it is likely to make the gospel a merely verbal gospel. As a preacher and teacher I'm always alone making tapes and standing behind lecterns and pulpits; but this is not where the message is to be found. Neither is the message in a book. In our day, we are comfortable with lecture-method Christianity, verbal Christianity, as if the truth could be an ideology, contained in words.

The most a preacher does is entice you, attract you, and call you out of yourself to live *a new kind of life*. But the gospel cannot happen in your head alone. You never think yourself into a new way of living. You invariably "live" yourself into a new way of thinking.

The gospel happens between two or more people. Unless there is someplace on this earth where it's happening between you and another person, I don't believe you have any criterion to judge whether it's happening at all. Unless you're in right relationship with at least one other person on this earth, unless there is someplace you can give and receive love, I don't think you have any reason to think you're "saved."

Salvation is not as antiseptic, unreal and sterile as we've made it. Just because I like to read the Bible and go to church services, "I'm saved." Is there at least one place in your life where you are giving and receiving love? If it happens in one place, it can happen everywhere. If you are truly capable of loving one person, you're capable of loving more than one, and eventually even your enemy, and finally *all*.

The converse is also true. Unless you are capable of loving in general, you can't love just one. That's an important realization for young people, because they start dating at sixteen and seventeen and get totally enthralled with this one other person. Observe a contemporary dating syndrome: They dress up and look their best, neat and cool, for one other person, but all the rest of the week they're down on everybody else. Negative, cynical, bitter to everyone else, but to their sweetheart they are positive, hopeful, and delighted: "Oh, I love you. You're so sweet and good." Unless you love in general, you can't love in particular. And until you love in particular, you don't know how to love in general.

Love is one piece. Thus, we rightly speak of being "in love" and Paul speaks of being "in Christ." In a way, love is all or nothing. You either express love or you don't. We can grow in our ability to be free and to understand ourselves, because they are skills to be learned and developed. But love is a gift of God. That's why when people first open up to the Spirit, open up to the love of God, it becomes hard for them to have uncharitable thoughts about other people or to harbor hatred in their hearts — because love and hatred have nothing in common. Darkness and light have nothing in common, and once love overtakes you, you simply can't sit around filled with hatred and bitterness any more. If you are, you're dealing with a great inconsistency in your being (see 1 John 1:5–7 and 4:20).

To be open to God's gift of love doesn't mean we're not tempted. Fleeting thoughts may come into us — impatience or dislike of another person — but we don't feed those thoughts and build on them. With love in our hearts, we find it hard to watch another person being torn down. And when we see love being violated, it does something in our guts. Love has taken over our lives, and there is no room for nonlove.

In sending out the disciples by twos, Luke is telling us that the gospel happens *between* people. It doesn't happen in your mind. That's called Gnosticism. I'd sooner say, if you have a sacrificial love for other people, you're saved. That is a much more valid test for the presence of the Spirit than "I am into religion."

He said to them, "The harvest is rich, but the laborers are few. So ask the Lord of the harvest to send laborers for his harvest" (10:2). Even in that time, there was a "vocation" problem, as we Catholics put it.

"Start off now, but remember, I'm sending you out like lambs among wolves" (10:3). Luke is reminding them there is no way this gospel is going to be easily understood or accepted. It will never have mass appeal. He gives them an honest but heroic image of their upcoming role.

"Carry no purse, no haversack, no sandals, salute no one on the road" (10:4). He's not saying to be unfriendly; he's just saying you have a focused purpose, a direction about your life. You see this in the life of the apostles. There's something we have to do, and we should be doing it. It also continues the theme of "mobile ministry," dependence and vulnerability. Luke is creating a world image here. In lines like, "Carry no purse, no haversack," Luke is creating a different mythic universe of "a simple people, free to be on the road."

Recently, I spent a week in Franciscan studies with my own community. Franciscan scholars are finding out that the rule of Francis is almost totally based on these scriptural missionary passages. Francis envisioned his order as a group of itinerant wanderers who, like Jesus, had no place to lay their head (9:58).

The rule of St. Francis could be called, "Tips for the Road" or "Life for Wanderers." Francis never presumed we would have houses we would call our own. He was telling us, "Don't tie into real estate and possessions. You can use things, but be ready to leave them tomorrow, to wander off somewhere else." There was great freedom and wisdom in such naiveté. Whatever house you go into, let your first words be, "Peace to this house." Shalom. If a man of peace lives there, your peace will go and rest on him (see 10:5–6).

Jesus is consoling the disciples. He knows how it hurts when you really try to be good to someone and you get rebuffed. You can just see a rejected disciple coming back to the missionary school sadly complaining. Jesus says, "You offer them your peace. You give them your love, your smile, your greeting. If they don't smile back, that's their problem." That would be our way of saying it. "Don't make their problem yours. You're so sensitive you feel rejected right away." He says, "Don't feel rejected; your peace will remain with you."

"Stay in that house, take what food and drink they have to offer. The missionary is worthy of his hire" (10:7). The world will take care of you. Certainly that's been my experience. I can't tell you how much kindness I've experienced in this country from coast to coast. Beautiful, beautiful people who literally take me in and do just what Jesus said. In fact, I usually put on three pounds each time I go out on the road, everybody is so good to me.

"Whenever you go into a town where they make you welcome, eat what is set before you. Cure those who are sick and say, 'The kingdom of God is very near to you' " (10:8–9). The primary way you say "The kingdom of God is near to you" is by your presence. As always, healing and preaching are combined, so much so that one could say there has been no real proclaiming of the kingdom unless there is healing in some real sense. It seems that Jesus and his Twelve took up residence in people's home and lived as close as possible to the people.

Many of us have sold out — understandably, necessarily — to an impersonal medium like the printed word. But the only way words can have any effect in your life is if a person is coming across through this medium. I have to try to give myself to you, to let you encounter me. That's the only experience that will make these words halfway believable. Jesus gave his "flesh" for the life of the world.

To the degree that the church becomes impersonal, it loses its power, because the incarnation is God's entrance into the personal. Whenever we move away from the personal, we move away from the power and the long-lasting experience of conversion. An impersonal or intellectual insight might generate a momentary conversion, a momentary high, but it doesn't last.

All of Jesus' rules of ministry here, his "tips for the road," are very interpersonal. They are based on putting people in touch with people. Person-to-person is the way the gospel was originally communicated. Person-in-love-with-person, person-respecting-person, person-forgiving-person, person-touching-person, person-crying-with-person, person-hugging-person: that's where the Spirit is so beautifully present.

Eddie Ensley, who wrote *Sounds of Wonder,* sent me a private monograph called *The Theology of the Kiss.* In it, he reported the doctors of the church saying amazing things that would never have been accepted later. These teachings came from way back in the second through the fourth centuries. Chrysostom, for example, said the kiss of peace was the vestibule of the Holy Spirit. Another said that in their community the baptism of the Holy Spirit was given in an embrace and a kiss. These early theologians were deeply in touch with their flesh and their personhood. They weren't afraid of it, as so many of us are. They understood the power of the interpersonal.

Restraint *and* passion — that is the paradoxical experience of the Holy. It takes time to learn that. You don't come to it by age twenty. You grow into the ability to love another in that way: to love one another in a way that totally gives yourself and entrusts yourself and yet respects that person and stands back.

So the seventy-two came back. *"Lord, even the devils submit to us when we use your name"* (10:17).

And he says (you can almost see the grin on his face), *"Yes, I watched Satan fall like lightning from heaven.* (Yes, boys, you're doing a good job. It's working, isn't it?) *I've given you power to tread under foot serpents and scorpions, and the whole strength of the enemy. Nothing shall ever hurt you. Yet do not rejoice that the spirits submit to you, rejoice rather that your names are written in heaven"* (10:18–20). "Don't rejoice about that power," Jesus says. "That's no proof that you're filled with the Holy Spirit." He says, "A lot of people are going to heal in my name, and that doesn't mean they're living the gospel."

That's forever hard for us to understand. It seems that once people submit to the gifts of God, once people open up to the charisma of God, God is faithful to those gifts. God maintains those gifts and allows people to keep using those gifts. But that is not necessarily holiness. Gifts — even healing itself — are not a sign or proof of holiness. Rejoice not in displays of power, but only in expressions of union — *"that your names are written in heaven"* (10:20).

The fruits of the Spirit are the only true signs of holiness, and that's what Jesus is saying in a context like this. Just because people do powerful things does not justify everything else they're doing. That warning applies to the Catholic Church and to all churches. Look instead for "love, joy, peace, patience, kindness, generosity, faithfulness, gentleness and self-control" (Gal. 5:22). This discernment of the presence of the Spirit will never be wrong. May this be helpful in your own discernment.

We notice a beautiful opening line reflecting Luke's gospel of joy in the Holy Spirit: *"Then filled with joy by the Holy Spirit,"* he said:

> *"I bless you Father, Lord of heaven and earth,*
> *for hiding these things from the learned and the clever*
> *and revealing them to mere children.*
> *Yes, Father, for that is what it pleases you to do."* (10:21)

Verse 21 might well have been taken from a hymn commonly sung in the early church because it appears almost identically in Matthew (Matt. 11:25). And the next part becomes one of the major themes in John's Gospel, the Father-Son mutuality that we participate: *"Everything has been entrusted to me by my Father and no one knows who the Son is except the Father and no one knows who the Father is except the Son"* (10:21–22).

"Turning to his disciples, he spoke to them in private" (10:23). It's interesting that Luke would have Jesus say the following words at this very point. *"Happy the eyes that see what you see"* (10:23). He has just given them the key to the door.

I think of a favorite phrase Franciscans often say to each other when we're with members of the community, "We're so lucky!" That's what Jesus is saying here. That's the sense of freedom and joy Luke wants his readers to feel. Most people search, suffer, and wait for this wisdom all their lives, they long for it and die for it and are not sure they have it together even at age sixty-two. And you've had the good news handed to you in your youth.

Even though the good news makes you happy, you still will have problems. But the difference is that with the gospel you have clear directions, a meaning system for your life so that you know how to deal with your pain — and allow all of it to become redemptive. We have met Someone who will transform and absorb all our wounds. We do not have to waste time in calculating, judging, accusing, or blaming. *"Many prophets and kings desired to see what you see, but did not see it, and to hear what you hear but did not hear it"* (10:24).

The Good Samaritan (Luke 10:29–37)

The story of the Good Samaritan, probably straight from Jesus, is so well known, that I won't reproduce it here. The question it seems to be answering for Luke's first readers is "Who am I required to love? Who belongs in our community?" In the story a lawyer poses the question in the form *"And who is my neighbor?"* (10:29) Jesus defines neighbor/membership at a very basic level. It is "The one who showed mercy." Jesus, in a kind of Socratic exchange, elicits the definition from the same lawyer who had asked the self-justifying question in a quick comeback to Jesus' simple statement of the great commandment (10:25–28).

In choosing to tell this story, Luke is saying the ones who belong in our church are those who take pity, who can live the compassionate life, who can live in love, who don't make divisions by race or theology. Jesus chooses someone outside the Jewish system — a Samaritan — to be the true neighbor.

It would be like one of us today asking the Lord, "Can Hindus be saved?" In response Jesus might create the following story: "One day this Catholic got attacked by a robber and was left on the road to die...." Probably in our context Jesus would say, "Now a Catholic priest came along and didn't pick him up. Then the head of the prayer group, the Levite, came along and also ignored the man. Then this old Hindu, who didn't obey the pope, didn't go to prayer meetings, and lacked training in Catholic theology, showed mercy on him, cared for him above and beyond the call of duty. He is, therefore, the true neighbor, and we must both imitate him and therein broaden our very notion of the community."

Jesus says there are those among us who show compassion, who have a broken heart, an open heart. These are the ones in the kingdom of God. Neighbor is not just your like-minded in-group.

The Good Samaritan story is a perfect statement of Luke's universal gospel. He focuses on the basics — pity, care, compassion — and doesn't get caught up in peripheral issues like religious denominations. Jesus is talking about the kingdom of God, not about religious sects. He leaves us no basis for ethnic hatreds or creating of victims. Instead, this amazingly anticlerical story puts the criticism back on the dominant and dominating group.

Martha and Mary (Luke 10:38–42)

In this uniquely Lucan passage Luke is making some points about discipleship and ministry. In the Mary and Martha story the Lord is not contrasting prayer and activism and putting primacy on a life of contemplation. Nor is the lesson that Martha should have prepared one casserole rather than half a dozen food courses. Rather he is saying the one prerequisite for being a follower of Jesus is listening to God's word. *Listening* is "the better part." And women can be just as good at that as men, because Mary has just broken into the all-male enclave that is discussing "theology" in the living room with Jesus.

Martha is trying to get Jesus to reinforce her cultural understanding of women's roles, and Jesus refuses to do it while still affirming Martha warmly. If you saw the movie *Yentl* (in which Barbra Streisand dresses like a man), you saw what lengths a woman had to go to study Torah. Jesus, against all his contemporaries and most Christians, has a very liberating and egalitarian approach.

Another important point in this story reflects Luke's gospel of women. Luke says Jesus *"came to a village and a woman named Martha welcomed him into her house"* (10:38). When Luke was writing his gospel, the nascent church was probably still meeting in people's homes; it was a time of "household Christianity," when women and families would host the church in their houses. This is an older tradition that we will probably be returning to in the coming years.

Luke 11

Chapter 11 begins with the Lord's Prayer. Since today we all use the same wording of the Lord's Prayer, we might think it was always that way. But in the early church there were at least two traditions of the Lord's Prayer, which means the prayer was probably recited differently in different Christian communities. Luke's concept and wording of the Lord's Prayer is much shorter and simpler than Matthew's (Matt. 6:9–13). Luke begins the prayer with "Father." He doesn't say, "Our Father who art in heaven," just, "Father."

The Lucan text is usually presumed to be the true, or at least the more primitive, text. Christian tradition, however, has chosen to follow the Matthew text, probably since it is longer, more developed, and has some embellishment to it. Most likely in Matthew's faith community that's the way they recited it.

We see how simple their theology of prayer is. The first statement, "Father (Abba)" defines their relationship to God. The use of that word in prayer marks a phenomenal breakthrough in the history of religion. It doesn't address God as "Judge," or "Divine Deity," or "Great Power in the Sky." Jesus tells his followers to address God as "Father." That's Christian theology in one word: *God is Father.* The emphasis is not God as male, however, but God as trustful caretaker. We know this because the characteristics that Jesus ascribes to this "Father" are qualities that most people would describe as "feminine." Unfortunately, most people have come to see God as masculine with a number of unintended results, most especially that the feminine face of God has been lost for many people.

I personally believe Jesus intentionally used the masculine word because it is the more hidden, the more scary, the more distant and daring word for most people. It is the area where we need the most healing and the most faith: to see that the masculine side of God is also *love* and *love-for-you.* That awareness is a breakthrough for most people, since most believe that the "mother" side of God is already for them.

It took humans a long time to "dare" to call God "Father." Scripture scholar Joachim Jeremias says that way of addressing God is a uniquely new contribution of Jesus. Jesus felt free to call God "Father" with all the good implications that flow from that name. Jeremias says that almost everything else Jesus taught can be found, at least in seed form in the Hebrew Scriptures (and really, *describing* God as Father can be found there in seed form, too) but the significant breakthrough Jesus makes is that he dares to *directly address God* as "Father" and carry that name to its logical conclusion of seeing himself as son.

"Father, may your name be kept holy" (11:2) is Luke's first line of the prayer. A synonym for the word holy is "other." Holiness is always otherness. When Luke says "holy," he's saying, "May we always remember that you are totally beyond us. You're totally great, totally other." That's why the Hebrews would not pronounce the divine name. In this way they preserved the transcendence of God. And we've got to remember that God, while totally with us, is also totally beyond us. "Your name is holy, you are beyond us."

The prayer is a calling for the coming of the kingdom. Every time we say the Our Father, we say, "Let the kingdom happen. Lord, let it happen." New Testament spirituality of prayer seems to be saying God cannot come into this world except by our invitation. Only as we say, "Come, Lord Jesus" and "Your kingdom come" can the Lord's power invade this world. That's why it's important that we keep saying, "Your kingdom come, your will be done. Whatever is happening in heaven, let it happen on earth."

Matthew's version develops this idea more fully. The most simple rule for discovering what we are to do on earth is to ask what's happening in heaven. What's happening in the heavenly kingdom is communion, unity, family. "Lord, your will be done on earth as it is happening in heaven." What God's love creates in heaven is perfect union. Union and communion are the goal of what God is doing on earth. God is not creating religion and righteousness; God is creating unity. Please remember that. So many people don't. God is about unity. That's why Jesus' basic rules for the kingdom are about forgiveness, reconciliation, healing, and communication. Those who are capable of union and communion are capable of God. Those not capable of communion, who are excommunicated, are not capable of God because they cannot share life, they cannot give and receive life or love. Our word for that state is "hell."

A paraphrase for the next phrase might be: "Give us each day our manna from heaven as you fed our forefathers in the desert." In 10:3 Luke is connecting his gentile Christians with the Jewish heritage, and teaching trust. The Exodus Hebrews watched the manna fall each day, and were supposed to gather up only enough for that day. If they tried to horde it or store it up for the future, it rotted. That's the significance of the *daily* bread. "Lord, we just live day by day. We trust you today. We know you'll take care of us today. Give us our bread today, and tomorrow we'll ask for it again." Twelve Step spirituality has discovered the same when it says, "One day at a time." Tomorrow we ask again for our daily bread, tomorrow we ask again that the kingdom come. The *daily* prayer of Christians keeps us both dependent and powerful at the same time.

"*Forgive us our sins*" (11:3). We stand as a people forgiven. That's essentially what Christians are: forgiven sinners. Not people who don't sin, but those who know they are forgiven, loved, and believed in. The very concrete practical corollary is that if we live in hatred and unforgiveness, we'll never be able to believe in God's forgiveness. Forgiving and being forgiven are two sides of one coin, so "forgive us our sins as we forgive one another."

When you find yourself incapable of forgiving another person, that means you're not standing in the stream of God's forgiveness. Work backward. When you find your heart hardened and you cannot forgive, you're forgetting that God forgives you. When you let your belief in God's forgiveness soften and free you, you find it easier to forgive others. As always, our truth is one truth.

"*Do not put us to the test*" (11:4). There have been many interpretations of this final petition. I don't find much agreement among scholars about what this line means. I like to interpret it as an admission of our weakness before God: "Lord, take care of us. Make it easy for us. We're weak. We can't take too much. We'll never make it." It's a parallel to the ancient and very popular Jesus Prayer, "Lord Jesus Christ, Son of God, have mercy on me a sinner."

Luke continues Jesus' teaching on prayer with passages that encourage patience, perseverance, and asking for the Holy Spirit, who not only teaches you how to pray but *actually is you praying.* The simplicity of the teaching reveals the heart of the problem. The only people I know who pray well are those who *continue* to pray. Perseverance is the only mark of "success" in prayer (11:5–13).

In Luke's Christian community, their school of missionaries held classes on prayer just as ours would today. There's no way you can be a disciple or missionary unless you are listening to God, in union with God, wasting time with God, letting go of the need to control and change things for a while. In prayer you're defined on your "being" level, not on your "having" level or "doing" level. Prayer happens at the level of being. If the world defines us on the level of doing and having, the Lord defines us on the level of being.

One's way of being can take many different forms as is clear in Luke's chapter on prayer. Don't tie yourselves down regarding prayer. People have different temperaments and different rhythms, and you have to discover how to pray according to your own rhythm and temperament.

I find many people very dissatisfied because of their unusual prayer lives. They always feel they are not doing it as they should. For some, perhaps, Tuesday afternoon from one o'clock to five is going to be their prayer time because during this particular time slot they can slow down, take off and drive to the country — or whatever it might be. For others, it is absolutely important to start every day with prayer. They just don't feel right all day if they don't get up early and spend half an hour in prayer. For some, prayer time is after supper; for others, it's after the kids are asleep or before they wake up in the morning. Still others take two days a month for retreat to saturate themselves with prayer. That doesn't mean they're not seeking communion with the Lord throughout the week.

There is no need to feel guilty about when, how, and how often you formally pray. As you understand your own temperament you will understand your way to pray. Those of us whose minds are always racing might need the Jesus Beads or the Rosary. (The Rosary was a stroke of genius — whoever invented it — Mary or Dominic or the medievals.) All repetition "leaves the mind barren" (1 Cor. 14:15) and thereby open to "another mind," as it were. Most religions have found ways to release people from the tyranny of their minds. "Peace of mind" is a common phrase but actually an oxymoron — you are either "at peace" or "in mind," but very seldom, if ever, *both* at the same time. "Doers," however, need liturgical prayer, where we can kneel, stand, sit, move around, eat, drink, and shake hands — that type of prayer. Walking meditation took the form of processions or the Stations of the Cross.

Those who are primarily "be-ers" may need a prayer of quiet. We may need charismatic and contemplative prayer forms that move beyond images. Or we may need prayer that employs our fantasy, imagination, and memory. I think those three faculties have been neglected in our spirituality tradition. In much Christian meditation, we tend to emphasize the faculties of our mind, exercising the memory, intellect, and will. Often we read our prayers from a printed page, which is probably fine for liturgical assemblies as long as it does not become an avoidance of spontaneous prayer from the heart. In the course of our lives we will likely move between these different prayer forms at different stages of our journey.

Jesus and Beelzebub

Some of the people wondered at the source of Jesus' power to cast out evil spirits. They said, *"It is through Beelzebub, the prince of devils that he casts out devils"* (11:15). Jesus answered, *"Every kingdom divided against itself is heading for ruin and a household divided against itself collapses. So too, with Satan: If he is divided against himself, how can his kingdom stand?"* (11:17–18) In this scene, it seems we are sitting in on a theological controversy, an ever-recurring discussion about personalized evil.

I think it is the undeniable teaching of Scripture and tradition that Satan exists. There is no way by any liberal theology that you can explain away this much Scripture and tradition and say Satan is simply a symbol for a psychological event or a projection of our sense of evil. On the other hand, of the many healings from evil spirits reported in the four gospels, I'm sure today we would treat some of them as psychological problems and others as physical or spiritual illness. Pope Paul VI acknowledged, "We have to sadly admit that the church knows very little about the world of evil spirits — after two thousand years." We're still for the most part in ignorance.

Again, this is an example of an area of concern where we haven't had good theology — and still don't. Today, instead of searching for a more adequate understanding of "evil spirits," we react cynically and throw everything out. Instead of trying to deal with satanic experience, we pretend it doesn't exist because it challenges us to enter another world that's frightening and unknown. Rather than venture into the unknown, we prefer not to deal with it at all. When the "shadow" is denied, however, it has free reign to expand.

I consider myself an educated person, but I too am embarrassed to talk about Satan. Yet, I've experienced too much to explain it away or dismiss it. I recognize in some people's lives a force, an obsession, a control that feels personal and demonic, and I've seen the Holy Spirit's power when we've prayed for deliverance and exorcism from evil spirits. I've seen a wildness, a contortion, and an absolute compulsion in people's lives, and the hatred of Satan toward us when we'd pray with such people. And I've seen the difference afterward. The exciting thing is to see the unbelievable power of Christ, the sacraments, and simple loving prayer.

The thread through all of this is the mystery of the incarnation. What the fathers of the church said, trying to explain the fall of Satan, was that Satan abhorred the idea of God becoming human — less than the angels. Satan could not accept the mystery of the incarnation: God submitting the divinity to lowly human estate.

Dealing with Satan involves fighting with this "angel" over material reality. In the sacramental system of the church, God manifests divine grace through water, bread, wine, oil. It's all incarnational. God has become incarnate — become flesh — and Satan tries to take possession of it. How does Satan do that?

We're not sure of all the tactics. More often it's obsession and oppression rather than possession. When someone has a personality weakness, some wounded area, say, feeling rejected or unlovable, that spiritual wound can sometimes be an opening for the Spirit of Rejection or the Spirit of Self-Hatred to enter.

On the other hand, a person raised in an environment of love, nurtured by others, the sacraments, and prayer, for the most part simply doesn't have a problem with satanic obsession. That again tells me the value of the church's support system. It's like a protective glass shield around you.

One other interesting point about evil spirits is there seems to be a military hierarchy among them. To read the medieval listings of demons is almost like the syllabus for a course in abnormal psychology. We would call it rightly "the discernment of spirits" (1 Cor. 12:10). For example, in the hierarchies of spirits the Spirit of Murder is one of the lower spirits, maybe a "sergeant." Do you know who his general is? *Bitterness.* People who give themselves over to the Spirit of Bitterness and feed on bitterness eventually might open themselves to the Spirit of Murder. (According to anthropologists, we now know there is a direct line from a culture of resentment to a culture of violence — and it sounds much more credible to say it that way!) It's usually some psychological wedge that we first open up to, some psychological defect or spiritual defect, whereby Satan gets into our mind to influence our attitudes and our spiritual world.

The same is true with sexual sins. We would think that, among sexual actions, adultery or premarital sex would be the bad one. No, the one at the top is the Spirit of Self-Hatred, of not believing we're lovable or loved. Once self-hatred takes over, we feel so unloved we need constant sexual confirmation that we're lovable. Then we give ourselves over to the sexual sins.

There seems to be an "order" to the work of love, as recent psychology is discovering, as well as an order to the work of evil. The evil spirits understand authority. It's amazing. This is being confirmed by contemporary thinkers like Ken Wilbur, who is reaffirming the hierarchical nature of the entire cosmos, and Bert Hellinger's landmark work on the "orders of love." That's what this dialogue or dispute in Luke 11 is about. "Where is your authority from, Jesus?" And Jesus stands on his union with God. "I am a son of the Father and I speak for him." When he stands on that authority, he is able to cast Satan out. *"If it is through the finger of God that I cast out devils, then know that the kingdom of God has overtaken you"* (11:20). Jesus understands and honors the orders of love and is willing to work effectively with the orders of evil. Then comes the line that contrasts with Luke 9:50. *"He who is not with me is against me and he who does not gather with me scatters"* (11:23). Jesus is not willing to compromise with any satanic power or be naive about its patterns.

I have often said that "most problems are psychological and most solutions are spiritual." Maybe that is a good practical summary of all teaching on deliverance. In a final note on deliverance (11:24–26), Jesus says, in effect, "After deliverance, when people are 'swept and tidied,' if you don't take care of them and provide some kind of support system by which the wound is fully healed and the fissure closed, Satan will reenter and the last state will be worse than the first." *"Seven worse spirits will reenter"* (11:26). We've discovered the truth of that teaching again and again. Many of the most alienated and cynical and disbelieving people I know are hurt priests, betrayed theologians, crushed idealists, former seminarians and religious women who have stopped believing but cannot leave.

The Core Mystery

"As he was speaking, a woman in the crowd raised her voice and said, 'Happy the womb that bore you, the breasts that you sucked.' But he replied, 'Still happier are those who hear the word of God and keep it' " (11:27–28). Again, Luke reminds us that Jesus has ex-

panded the notion of family. He's not denigrating his mother; in fact, you can almost picture, as he speaks, Jesus making eye contact with Mary standing in the crowd and winking at her, saying, "You know you're one of them. If anybody knows the will of God, it is you, Mom. But I have to say this to teach the people."

This "hearing and keeping" of the Word of God is now brilliantly illustrated by what appears to be a central metaphor for Jesus: "the sign of Jonah" (11:29–32). He says that it is the *only* sign that he is going to give! (Take note, seekers of miracles, apparitions, and healings.)

He seems willing to offend the "even bigger" crowd in front of him and says it is "an evil generation that wants signs," something that I myself would be afraid to say. Yet it is clear that Jesus is now clarifying the core of his message, *the* mystery of faith. Augustine later called it the "paschal mystery" and it is the constant theme of every Eucharist to this day: "Christ has died, Christ is risen, Christ will come again." If you don't get this, you just don't get it.

Without the sign of Jonah — the pattern of new life *only* through death ("in the belly of the whale") — Christianity remains a largely impotent ideology, another way to "win" instead of the pain of faith. Or it becomes a language of ascent instead of the treacherous journey of descent that characterizes Jonah, Jeremiah, Job, John the Baptizer, and Jesus. After Jesus, we Christians used the metaphor "the way of the cross." Unfortunately, it became "what Jesus did to save us" — or a negative theology of atonement — instead of *the necessary pattern that is redemptive for all of us.* Jesus became the cosmic problem-solver instead of the teacher of the path.

This one great truth has also been discovered by what we call Eastern religions: Taoism, yin and yang philosophy, the detachment of Buddhism, the Hindu god of destruction and regeneration, Shiva. It is utterly surprising and disappointing that so many Christians think they are discovering this mystery for the first time in new religions. The Jonah-Job-Jesus pattern has been hard for Westerners to recognize and accept. There was probably a cultural resistance to it in the Greco-Roman West where we were always into ascending and continual progress. The sign of Jonah is at the heart of the matter and, not surprisingly, leads to a short teaching by Jesus on darkness and light (11:33–36).

Chapter 11 ends with a condemnation of legalism, which is what always recurs when you don't submit to the vagaries of the sign of Jonah. It is very similar to Matthew's condemnation of legalism in chapter 23, condemning the Pharisees and the scribes. In this regard, we continue to show an altogether amazing capacity for not getting the point. The pattern continues at the highest levels of the church as we lose our grip on real influence and control. (This section is being written at Louvain University in Belgium after two weeks of reports on the devastated state of the church in Europe, and three weeks of preaching to discouraged Catholics in Northern Europe.) *"A lawyer spoke up. 'Master,' he said, 'when you speak like this you insult us too'"* (11:45). A necessary insult, it seems, because Jesus only gets stronger (see 11:47–54) and condemns the "lawyers" again and again! Those preoccupied with "orthodoxy" will find these verses hard to comprehend.

Luke 12

As chapter 12 begins, Luke has Jesus giving consolation to the returning missionaries. They've probably been persecuted in some places, and he says, *"Do not be afraid of those who kill the body and after that can do no more"* (12:4). He's giving them the vision of the whole. He's getting them up there on Thérèse's cloud, saying, "Look at the whole picture. Don't worry about your body, your body is not you." That theme fills much of the rest of chapter 12: Your body is not you. You're more than a physical thing. Your body is part of you, but it does not control you. Do not worry, therefore, about what you are to wear or eat (see 12:22).

In the middle of chapter 12, Luke creates a scene where two men are arguing about property and money, *"Master, tell my brother to give me a share in our inheritance"* (12:13). Jesus refuses to get into these kind of arbitrations. *"My friend, who appointed me your judge?"* (12:14). He says, in effect, "I'm not going to get caught up in picayune moral decisions, but I will tell you a story."

"There was once a rich man, who having had a good harvest from his land, thought to himself, 'What am I to do? I have not enough room to store my crops. This is what I will do. I will pull down my barns and build bigger ones'" (12:16–18). In modern terms the man might say, "I'll open a checking account in addition to my savings account and start a third account in another bank."

Jesus continues: *"Then the man says to himself, 'My soul, you have plenty of good things laid up for many years to come. Eat, drink, take it easy. Have a good time.' But God said, 'Fool, this very night demand will be made for your soul'"* (12:19–20). Jesus is saying, "You are more than what you possess. You are not just your body, you're more than what you have. You are what you are. And that, no one can take from you." Jesus answers the brothers' specific moral question by telling this story about greed. He says, "Don't sit around worrying about how much of your parents' inheritance you're going to get, because that doesn't matter in the full and final state of affairs."

This situation has its modern parallels. You remember the old system where Catholics loved to ask priests questions? The questions we used to ask weren't about inheritances, but usually about sex. The questions were about "How far could we go sexually without committing sin?" or "What actions were mortal or venial sins?" That's the self-preoccupied kind of questions they're asking here. Jesus always refuses to answer such questions because they are the wrong questions and proceed from the self as a reference point. (In fact, Jesus hardly ever answers any questions directly.)

Now if priests had been wise in those days, they would never have answered such questions. But they did. Or they tried to. What they should have done is what Jesus did: tell a story, a parable of the kingdom. "Listen, if you're living at that petty level, you don't really understand. Brother, if you knew the world was going to end one month from today, what would you do right now? What would really matter to you? Would you spend the last few weeks of your life being concerned about sex, success, status, degrees, and fame? You know what you'd probably do? By phone, mail, or in person, you'd tell as many people as you could one or all of three things: 'I'm sorry' or 'I love you' or 'I forgive you.' That's what you'd do for this last month. That's what life's all about. That's the kingdom: *to live now what matters forever.* That's the freedom of the kingdom: to live today your final state of affairs."

"Live now what matters in eternity," is Jesus' message. Live on earth what's happening in heaven. He says in effect, "Don't ask me any more about how far you can go and when, or what action constitutes a mortal sin? I'm not going to waste your time and mine with those misleading questions. They only delay the needed and new perspective."

The way Jesus usually answers questions is by telling a story. There is creative and healing power in a story. It doesn't avoid the question, but goes to the root of the question. A lot of people don't like that approach, because it doesn't seem clear or objective enough. But in fact that's the way the great masters of religion always taught — by simply telling stories, and giving the soul room to grow and understand.

"Set your hearts on his kingdom and all these other things will be given you as well. There is no need to be afraid, little flock, for it has pleased your Father to give you the kingdom" (12:31–32). Jesus is in effect telling us, "Stop working for the kingdom, you've already got it. Stop trying to achieve it, it's already yours. Don't try to work for gifts. If you do, they're not gifts. The Lord has given you his kingdom already. Stop trying to get saved, you're saved already. Insofar as you believe it each moment, insofar as you let it happen, you will experience it."

That's why the call is to faith, to believe. Such faith is the opposite of anxiety. Without such faith you are necessarily going to be concerned with management and security questions. If God isn't *for you*, you must be self-preoccupied. In fact, you would be irresponsible not to be! As soon as you stop believing in a loving God, you revert to yourself. The gospel has freed us from groveling before God or trying to earn God's approval. We all have that approval already. God loves us — unconditionally.

If you have this attitude, it is easy to understand what Jesus says next: *"Sell your possessions. Give alms. Get yourselves purses that do not wear out, treasure that will not fail, in heaven, where no thief can reach it or no moth destroy it. For where your treasure is, there will be your heart be also"* (12:33–34). The simplest rule of thumb for each of us is to ask "Where do we spend our time and where do we spend our money?" That's where our treasure is, we can be sure. The focus of your time and money will tell you what your God is and what is important in your life. As others have wisely said, your checkbook and your calendar reveal your true belief system.

Then comes the call to be awake (12:35–48), to be ready for the master's return, to live life in the present. Jesus is *not* calling us to be afraid of God or warning us about God. Jesus is *not* saying, "God's right around the corner and is out to get you." Rather he is warning us about missing life. He is saying, "It's all right here and now. Live in the moment and don't let life just float you along. Choose life each moment. Enjoy it each moment. Live it each moment." In Catherine of Sienna's words, "It's heaven all the way to heaven, and hell all the way to hell."

We have a Jewish brother in the community who had been totally raised in Judaism. When he first came, he said in all simplicity, "What my Rabbi told me was that God gave us everything to enjoy and we're going to be judged on how much we enjoyed it."

I said, "Oh, you're so free. That's wonderful. Please teach that to us Christians. We've lost that sense of freedom." He said, "God gave us everything to enjoy, really enjoy." What a wonderful possibility.

To know how to enjoy takes a lot of discipline as well as a lot of restraint. Pleasure and joy are not the same. God did not create us simply for pleasure; he created us for joy, which is all-embracing, deep, enduring, steady. To live in joy is the gift of the Spirit. We have to be a people who once again are free to enjoy — to enjoy our lives, to enjoy our selves, to enjoy one another. For a lot of us that means a healing of our emotional life.

"Emotionally intelligent" people can look at the world very objectively and at the same time very subjectively. That's the synthesis, the genius — when you can look at reality objectively, as it is really happening, and not just project yourself onto it; and at the same moment, you can look at things very subjectively, very personally. You can tell when someone's down, when someone's hurt or angry, out of it, or rejected. You take all that in, and then you know how to respond to it. Now read Luke 12:35–48 and see if you can't hear it with entirely new ears. It is not a threat about the future but an invitation to live *now*.

Jesus is a cause of dissension. If the missionaries in Luke's community create dissension in the towns where they bring the good news, they should know that it happened to Jesus, too. *"Do you suppose that I am here to bring peace on earth? No, I tell you, rather, division"* (12:51). It is significant that all of the examples used are "vertical" relationships of dominance and submission, superiority and inferiority. Clearly Jesus' teaching is upsetting to the social order.

"From now on, a household of five will be divided" (12:52). The missionaries in Luke's community are coming back and saying, "Listen, there's a family over there in the next town that has broken up because of our gospel. The kids are all turned on but the parents don't like them going to the prayer meeting, and we don't know what we should do." But in another place (10:6), Luke had Jesus say just the

opposite. *"Whatever house you go into, let your first words be, 'Peace to this house.'"* In each case, he's talking to a different missionary situation.

Similarly, he tells them in verse 12:54 to *"read the signs of the times."* This was the scriptural verse that the Second Vatican Council emphasized. The church has to start reading the signs. Get your antennae out and listen to what's happening in people's hearts. He says, *"When you see a cloud looming up in the West, you say that rain is coming, and so it does. When the wind is from the South you say it will be hot, and so it is. You can read the face of the earth and the sky. How is it you can't interpret these times?"* (12:55–56).

Jesus is clearly telling us that his message will need application and transitioning to new situations. That's who we should be, people who can read not only the sky but culture, trends, and situations. That takes a lot of listening — and sometimes a lot of study and conversation. Travel helps a lot, too, because it provides additional points of comparison. When reading the signs of the times is no longer valued, we have misinterpretation of events, and fear normally dominates the scene. Then we rush to dominative uses of power to get everything under control (when it is really our own fear we are trying to control).

This call to both study and common sense ends with a call to individual formation of conscience. Not surprisingly, this quote is not often referred to by the institution. *"Why not judge for yourselves what is right?"* he says (12:57). He's telling them, "You do have the gift of knowledge. Use it." We do Jesus, the church, and the gospel no favor when we avoid the formation of adult and intelligent Christians. The management mind wants efficiency and control. The Jesus mind is willing to call and wait for true holiness. They are two very different agendas and we have heard the better one here.

Luke 13

Jesus says, "Do you suppose these Galileans who suffered like that were greater sinners than any other Galileans? They were not, I tell you" (13:2–3). We can suppose that the missionaries in Luke's community are returning home with the age-old question, "Why do bad things happen to good people?" People still ask priests and missionaries this question today. People still struggle with this problem in their gut. "My son died. God doesn't love me. What did I do wrong? Why is God punishing me because my child is taken away from me?"

In our guts most of us still think that way. When something really bad happens, we believe God did it. But we often do not give God credit for the good. What does that say about our notion of God? At any rate, Jesus breaks the fatalistic connection. Luke is quoting Jesus speaking to his missionaries. *"Or those eighteen on whom the Tower at Siloam fell and killed them? Do you suppose they were more guilty than all the other people living in Jerusalem? They were not"* (13:4).

In other words, Jesus is saying, "Don't try to put a strict cause-and-effect relationship between people who suffer or people having a hard time, and God doing it to them. It doesn't happen that way. In great part, reality takes its course by the movement of the times and seasons and the sins of human beings. Reality just keeps on going. And God is used to writing straight with crooked lines.

To those who call upon God in faith, to those who trust in God, God's power can be channeled through their lives to bring good into the world: to heal, change, and transform events and people. But where saints are not present, where people who are open to God are unavailable, there is no clear channel of God's presence in the world. Nature, changes of times, and sinners largely direct the course of this world. But the leaven of saints, the "ten just men," are enough to keep the world from self-destruction.

What Jesus seems to be saying is that God didn't push over that tower at Siloam to punish those eighteen people. The tower fell because the bricks were crumbling on one side. He says, "Those of you who can find God in all things, you're going to bring good out of that bad experience. But unless you "repent," you also will perish (13:5). Those who don't know how to listen, wait, and hope will view such an event simply as a destructive experience. It's by your faith, by your perspective, your trust and hope and prayer, that you bring good out of evil. Otherwise evil will take its course in the world. What we see happening in our time — perhaps in all times — is that the course of evil is becoming overwhelming. It seems to be overtaking the world. As John puts it, Satan is the real "prince of the world" (14:30).

God only gets in through the cracks, it seems, the cracks in our hearts, the now and then openings in history, the wounded and broken ones who long for God. Leonard Cohen says, "There is a crack in everything, and that's how the light gets in." Maybe faith is the accepting of that crack.

For Jesus, parables are just punch-line answers to the question: "What is the kingdom of God like?" Most of Jesus' parables are dealing with that basic question. To what shall I compare the kingdom of God? There are several good parables/images in this chapter.

The parable of the mustard seed (13:18–19) is good for people who want the kingdom to happen right now — they want to be holy after their first year on the journey. For the kingdom to happen, we have to walk the whole journey. The kingdom is like a mustard seed. It starts small, but it keeps growing. So keep growing. As time goes on you'll sprout many branches, and you'll look out at the end of your life and you'll say, "God has done it. God has been faithful to the promise. God has made beauty out of my little life." This is process spirituality, which mirrors the salvation history of the Bible itself. Mustard seed spirituality is realistic, humble, patient, and honest.

As is the next image of the leaven. To what shall I compare the kingdom of God? *"It is like the yeast a woman took and mixed with three measures of flour until eventually it was all leavened through"* (13:21). This is hardly static, born-again theology. Salvation is a process, a leavening of the dough as God slowly converts us, frees us, and liberates our hearts. It is rather hidden, and yet you know when it is not there. You don't ever see yeast but there is no risen bread without it. The images of God as housewife and baker seem to have had less influence than the images of God as king and judge.

At the end of chapter 13, Jesus addresses Jerusalem. *"You that killed the prophets and stoned those who were sent to you. How often have I longed to gather your children as a hen gathers her brood under her wing"* (13:34). Psychologists find this very maternal feminine image interesting. Surprisingly, Luke's Jesus uses much more feminine imagery than masculine. Somewhere in Jesus' life he was in good relationship with a woman or he could not have been that comfortable with feminine perspectives or feminine imagery.

Men who have never had good experiences with women tend to become very macho, very rational, very controlling, cold. On the other side, a woman who has never enjoyed a good relationship with a man tends to become overemotional, saccharine or sentimental, and constantly up and down.

So we see Jesus here using this hen image, speaking of himself as a hen and us as little chicks. (St. Francis uses this same imagery and other very feminine imagery too.) This is not a slick, hard-hitting business approach to religion. Jesus offers a very familial, personal approach, with a masculine/feminine complementarity. He understands how people grow and how people are fed and set free. Images of family and relationships are the most sexually charged and, finally, the most transformative.

It's interesting that he would apply the mother hen image to himself. It's never been taken up by art. (Maybe it's too hard to do.) So many other animals mentioned in the Scriptures — lambs, lions, eagles — have been used in Christian art through the centuries to symbolize Jesus, but this beautiful image of the Lord as a hen and us as the chicks has not. There's something really exquisite about this imagery. I'm sorry it has not ever been developed.

Luke 14

Chapter 14 is focused around tables and table-fellowship. Luke begins with Jesus going for a meal to the house of one of the leading Pharisees; Luke notes that all of the guests watch Jesus closely (14:1–2). In that "hostile" context Luke has Jesus tell three little stories about: choosing places at table (14:7–11), choosing guests (12–14), and invited guests who make excuses (15–24).

Luke remembers and gathers together in one place three stories (there are ten in his whole gospel) that seem to have something to do with Jesus sitting at a table. Eating together or having dinners with guests must have been a common occurrence in Jesus' ministry. For him, the table is the place of fellowship and communion. It is also the place where he redefines the social order by doing things differently and usually upsetting those who are in control of the social order — the rich, the elders, the scribes, and the "politically correct." It is now accepted by most biblical scholars that table fellowship seems to have been Jesus' unique form of visual sermon, cultural critique, and social protest. He seems to have invented the "sit-in." In these stories Luke is answering the question: Whom do you invite to share the meal with you? "Who can be a part of our faith community? Is there an 'in' group and an 'out' group?"

First addressing the host, he answers: Do not invite only your friends and family or rich neighbors, who can repay you. *"No, when*

you have a party, invite the poor, the crippled, the lame and the blind"
(14:13). Jesus is saying, "In the new universal order, we're going to
have to forget the status symbols of the world. Human hierarchies
mean nothing to God. What matters is simply our common humanity
and the desire to be in communion."

Today we may claim, "Oh, we're beyond that." But in our own
subtle prejudicial ways, we Christians still have exclusive criteria for
membership. We've seen them lasting into our time. Some can remember when blacks had to sit at the back of Catholic churches in
this country. That's happened within our own lifetime. Maybe you
know other examples of prejudicial treatment in the church from your
own parts of the country. Divorce and remarriage is one failure that
continues to be singled out as making one unworthy for membership.

When I was in the West Indies, I noticed all along the front of
the church sat the aristocracy of the island. Those front pews were
padded. The others sat in back on unpadded pews. Expressions of
privilege do hold on. We humans like to create divisions. We love to
feel that one group is more important than another. Jesus is dismiss-
ing such practices, saying they have no place in the kingdom of God.
In fact, to use Paul's phrase, "It is the least honorable parts of the body
that we clothe with the greatest care" (1 Cor. 12:23). Now that is a
new world order!

We clergy created divisions in our own way too. For example, in
the construction of the communion rail, we created two groups: we
permitted only the clergy on one side of the rail, the laity on the
other. In the New Testament we certainly don't find rails that separate
groups. Instead we find ministering people. This distinction between
the separated ones — the clergy who dress differently, for example —
is certainly hard to justify by the New Testament. Yet, most Christian
denominations are still very comfortable with that distinction today.

We perpetuate a similar separation in the distinction between men
and women, rich and poor, gay and straight, fit and handicapped,
Christian and non-Christian. If anything, Jesus is giving the head start
to the outsider in almost all of his parables. "In Christ there is no distinction between Jew and Greek, male and female, between slave and
free, but all are one in Christ Jesus" (Gal. 3:28).

After addressing the hosts, he goes on to address the would-be
guests. Even if there were no separations, Luke realizes that the call
inviting people to the table is constantly refused (14:15–24). Many do

not know the gift of God. Many do not appreciate what they have been called to. So Luke presents this powerful set of excuses that are familiar to all of us. And they're always very good excuses, righteous and understandable. What newlyweds would want to go somewhere else and not prefer to be by themselves? Who would not want to pull their oxen out of a ditch — or care for their auto if it had a breakdown?

The would-be guests are like the elder son in the prodigal son story (which soon follows). They don't know the gift that they have and don't want to bother going to the banquet. The master uses this as a lead-in to the guests who actually come: *"the poor, the crippled, the blind and the lame"* (v. 21). Today, we call this the "preferential option for the poor." The little ones seem to have a head start, a symbolic advantage in understanding Jesus' message and invitation. I have no doubt this is true, especially after many years of preaching to the folks in the so-called Third World. Jesus seems to be saying *they* are in the First World spiritually.

Understandably, Luke then delivers this powerful and troublesome line: *"If any man comes to me without hating his father, mother, wife, children, brothers, sisters, yes and even his own life, he cannot be my disciple. Anyone who does not carry his cross and come after me cannot be my disciple"* (14:26–27). This is obviously a teaching to a later development of the Christian community. It could hardly have come from the mouth of Jesus, since carrying *his* cross hadn't happened yet. This is later Christian imagery. After Jesus carried his cross, it became a familiar phrase in the community — "to carry your cross" — and so Luke put that phrase anachronistically in the mouth of Jesus.

The Lord is never afraid to put things in a hard way, and Luke knows this passage might be needed after this talk about who is at the banquet. He's not afraid of using a word that's inevitably going to be misunderstood. He puts his truth out there; dealing with it is the listener's problem. He is saying, in effect, "Struggle with what I'm saying!" In general, Jesus doesn't spend a great deal of time qualifying his point and making sure everybody understands it clearly. He presents a teaching and it's our problem to find the truth that's there. He often puts a burden on us. As a good preacher he knows that if you qualify too much, your word loses its power. You can end up explaining everything away. Actually, speaking in unqualified language is the secret power of the fundamentalist preacher, the power someone like me loses because I explain everything. When you just put your message out in black and white, it possesses a power — albeit a dangerous and often misused one.

Now such language doesn't deal with the subtleties of life and it can lay guilt on people, but that's a secondary problem. What's primary is that it does call to faith. The way Jesus preaches is to just present the story or the saying, and you the listeners have to deal with it yourselves. Because Jesus didn't qualify, he must have had the usual crowd out there, saying, "I don't know if I agree with that statement" or "What did you mean by this word?"

The point of evangelical preaching is to call listeners to a version of faith and to give the Word a concrete application. It's hard to do both. This may suggest a legitimate distinction between preaching and teaching. Preaching puts out the word with immediacy and concreteness, calling to decision; it doesn't deal with all the intricacies and qualifications. Teaching, on the other hand, says, "What Jesus meant when he told this parable...," or an equivalent; it deals with all the subtleties. You need both preaching and teaching in a Christian community.

Preaching is an important gift that we as Catholics have poorly developed. Protestantism at one end of the spectrum often has nothing but evangelism, while Catholics don't even know what evangelists are. Why can't the denominations come together into the healthy middle? I think we're trying to do that.

In 14:28 Luke addresses the renunciation of possessions. Luke uses every chance he can to bring up this issue. It's a hard teaching for us to hear today. If some of you were not born Christian and you simply picked up a document like Luke to read, without any previous prejudices, would you really see in the teaching of this man a philosophy of life that you would choose for yourself? Would you say, "This is the word of the Lord" and "Thanks be to God"? I don't think I would. I think Luke's message would be deeply threatening to most, especially to affluent Americans.

Try to look at Luke's teaching simply and objectively. If you were to select one book and say, "This is going to be the philosophy of my life," I doubt if most of us would choose Luke's Gospel, because it hits us too deeply in areas where we're quite comfortable, myself included. He ends the chapter with an impossible one-liner: *"None of you can be my disciple unless he gives up all his possessions"* (v. 33). Now what do we do with that? In general, I would say Jesus seems to want to draw his listeners into "conversations that matter" as opposed to offering quick closure and snug answers. Those conversations expose our real loyalties and offer us wider and creative horizons.

Luke 15

In chapter 15, Luke ties together three parables of God's mercy. According to his typical writing style, when he begins a new theme, he'll gather together a series of images and stories related to it.

The lost sheep is an interesting image (15:4–7). It is also an example of how the same story is remembered and used for two different purposes by different authors. If you refer to Matthew (18:12–14), he tells the same story but his punch line is about preaching to the church — to ministers. Matthew is saying, "It is never the will of the Father that even one of these little ones should be lost" (Matt. 18:14). He's talking about the importance of the individual and how ministers should be concerned about each individual.

Luke takes the same story and makes it a teaching on mercy. *"I tell you, there will be more rejoicing in heaven over one repentant sinner than over ninety-nine virtuous ones who have no need of repentance"* (15:7). He does the same with the second story of the lost coin (15:8–10).

The same oral tradition of the gospel carried the story of the lost sheep, but different evangelists interpreted it differently. Matthew taught us about ministry, Luke about mercy and forgiveness. I think it's valuable to see this difference in interpretation. Matthew and Luke didn't call one another unorthodox and say, "You can't say that. This story means this and only this." They're both true mythic writers. They understand the same story or image can have two meanings — and even more — and we don't have to call the other person a heretic.

Whenever you start using the word "only" — "It can mean *only* this" — you start limiting your theology. Keep your doors open. Someone might present a third interpretation of the lost sheep story, and it might mean that too. One understanding of a story doesn't mean it can't have other interpretations. God will use the divine Word to teach many different things to us. So beware of a theology that keeps saying "only."

After the story of the lost sheep and lost coin comes the story we've always called the Prodigal Son (15:11–32). This is not the best title. It might better be called the story of the two sons. It seems the story was told, first of all, to present the attitude of the elder son as the image of the usual church person: the obedient person, the good Jew. Luke presents him as "the one who never disobeyed your orders" (v. 29) but who will not come to the banquet.

The Prodigal Son might also be better called the story of the Merciful Father. It's a proclamation of the nature of God's love and mercy. It's interesting that we've emphasized the prodigal son, because he is the least important of the characters here. He's not the Everyman figure. We're all certainly prodigal sons, but the real Everyman figure Luke is concerned with is the righteous church person who get upset at people who get saved after they've lived a whole life of sin.

"How can they be as good as I am? I've been going to Mass faithfully since I've been six years old. I always obey the law. And now these people come along being converted and dancing in the Spirit at age sixty, while I had to suffer all my life. Didn't my faithfulness get me any points with God?" In that context, God as the only faithful one becomes very apparent. God as the merciful father is clearly the protagonist and hero of the story.

The African missionary I keep speaking about told me he found stories like the prodigal son in many African cultures. He told one from the tribe among whom he was working. He said it almost brought tears to his eyes when he first understood it, as it did to me.

In this tribe, I believe it is the Massai tribe, the father-son relationship is absolutely essential to the perpetuation of the culture. In no way can that relationship be tampered with or destroyed, or everything falls apart. The son has to be faithful to his father and the father has to be faithful to his son. When this faithfulness is broken, there is one unwritten rule which every father understands. If the son breaks the relationship, leaves his home or is mad at his father, the father does one thing immediately. He goes to the mountains to pray. He remains in prayer asking God for the "spittle of forgiveness."

First of all, observe the psychology at work here. Imagine the son out eating the husks of corn or whatever he is doing, knowing for certain that his father is praying. We have nothing like this in our culture. He *knows* his father is praying and is going to stay up in the mountains until the two of them are reunited. That reconciliation has got to happen. The father and the son have to be in unity.

The father remains in the mountains, praying for the spittle of forgiveness. This says something important about sacramentalism, for when the son does decide to return home after he's sown his wild oats or rebelled or whatever, then runners go to the mountain to tell the father his son is returning. These runners accompany the father down the mountain, and another contingent accompanies the son. The tribe's whole life is ritualized. Everything is sacramental. Because we are not a sacramental people, life is no longer ritualized for us. But for community-centered cultures, their ritual is all set up. It's never broken.

Here are the two teams coming together, the father with the runners coming down from the mountain and the other contingent coming with the son. They meet and, of all things, what the father does is spit on his son's face. Among us, that would be a sign of contempt. For them, it is giving to the son what is from inside the father, the spit which symbolizes himself. The running of the father's spit over the son's face is their deepest symbol of forgiveness. Throughout this culture, spit is constantly used as a symbol of forgiveness.

Now the American priest came along and was supposed to say that forgiveness happens inside a dark box when you say, "I did this three times," and the priest says, "You are forgiven." The missionary explained, "That symbolism doesn't mean anything there, so I had to create a rite based on the spittle of forgiveness to communicate the meaning of reconciliation." That's the deep kind of sacramentalism we have to work for, especially in a culture that already knows how to speak forgiveness.

We're lucky today. In our new approach to the sacrament of reconciliation looking and touching are encouraged. Hugs are possible. That's the kind of rituals we need to have forgiveness communicated to us — some kind of look of love, some kind of understanding expression, human warm touch, bodily encounter, perhaps an embrace. We can't keep doing it with more and exact words.

I use that African story as another example of the same kind of story Jesus is trying to tell here in the parable of the two sons. Jesus uses the precious relationship between the father and the son as an image of the God/person relationship. Most commentators agree that this story expresses the true spirit and style of the historical Jesus. In this quintessential Jesus sermon, he is saying that God takes the initiative, God is the lover, God loves unconditionally, God knows we've sinned, but God comes running out after us. It would be a very different gospel and different church history if we didn't have this larger-than-life-and-death story found only in Luke.

Luke 16

The problematic parable of "the crafty steward" (16:1–8) has God recommending "trickster" theology (making the best of bad things). It is a good introduction to a problematic chapter on money, marriage, heaven, and hell. First, we get into some hard words on money. *"No servant can be the slave of two masters. He will either hate the first and love the second, or treat the first with respect and the second with scorn. You cannot be the slave of both God and money"* (16:13). When Father Rick Thomas preaches — he lives among the dumps of Juarez — he'll just take the phrase and say it fifteen times. "You cannot serve God and money." He says it over and over, then walks away. It's his entire sermon. Of course, because he's living the life of the poor who have to trust in the Lord, he has the right to preach it.

"The Pharisees, who loved money, heard all this and laughed at Jesus. He responded, 'You are the very ones who pass yourself off as righteous in people's sight, but God knows your heart. For what is thought of highly by men is loathsome in God's eyes'" (16:14–15). Luke is doing everything he can to turn the system upside down. Jesus presents an either/or worldview here. It is the style used when a teacher is calling you to make a choice, to get off the fence, or to recognize a false choice you have already made.

Next we have a collection of little teachings about the law, even one on marriage. *"Everyone who divorces his wife and marries another is guilty of adultery, and the man who marries a woman divorced by her husband commits adultery"* (16:18). This is the very hard teaching from the earliest oral tradition. It is found in all the four gospels. Yet, as I pointed out, we see already a development of doctrine where both Matthew (5:32) and Paul are willing to make exceptions (see 1 Cor. 7:12–16). This is interesting and very important for our usage of Scripture and for our appreciation of the Holy Spirit in the history of doctrine.

Certainly our goal, our ideal, our basic plan for marriage is that it is indissoluble and forever. Yet we are dealing with the unbelievable complexity of human relationships. To describe a divorce situation to-

day, the image I like to use is trying to unscramble scrambled eggs. It is
so difficult to say what God would want in each situation, or what is
going to bring about the greatest good, or what is going to bring about
the spirit of Jesus in the life of the Body of Christ. All I can say to those
of you who are struggling with the divorce question and find a gospel
statement like this so hard is that you'll have to take it to prayer, then
submit yourselves to wise and holy men and women who can listen to
you and lead you to the wisdom that is the will of God for you.

There is no doubt that an indissoluble marriage is the ideal and the
goal. Yet we see that Paul and Matthew have already come to understand that we have to respect ideals and work toward them, but ideals
aren't achieved just by insisting on them. How do we at least preserve
the values inherent in the ideals? That is the more important question.

What is marriage in Christ? What does it mean to be married in the
Lord? It isn't simply because you got married in St. Agnes Church.
That's why it is like unscrambling scrambled eggs. There are some
people who didn't get married in St. Agnes Church who might well
be married in the Lord, and there are some people who did get married in St. Agnes Church who are probably not married in the Lord.
Christian marriage isn't the black-and-white situation we've made it.
Canon lawyers at the marriage tribunal find they have to deal with
each situation individually: where this man is at, where that woman
is at, and where their relationship has been. This takes a lot of prayer
and listening, a lot of waiting.

The great problem in ministry today is that we don't have the wise
people — spiritual directors, people with breadth and depth of knowledge — to help confused spouses discern these kind of things and call
them to faith decisions on either side. I personally believe couples can
stay together without love and faith and couples can painfully decide
to divorce with great love and faith. The law cannot always resolve
our inability to live out our ideals. We would do better to offer rituals of separation, forgiveness, healing, and sending than annulment
courts (in my humble opinion).

The story of the rich man and Lazarus is obviously a mythic story.
It has all the forms of a more primitive source, since the characters are
archetypal and the images are grandiose and universal. The "bosom
of Abraham" has become salvation. It's one of the few parables where
personal names are given. The name Dives is simply the Latin word
for riches. Lazarus is not likely the same Lazarus spoken of in John's

Gospel. Hades, or Sheol, is the abode of the dead. It doesn't coincide with our term "hell" because everybody who has died is there. There is a big wall or chasm between the two sides. The dead whom God likes are on one side and the dead whom God doesn't like are on the other. This imagery is the beginning of the development of what later in Christian thinking became heaven and hell. But at this stage, Hades is simply the abode of the dead. At any rate, the story offers another chance for Luke to console the poor and critique the rich, and to say you can't have it both ways.

Luke is dealing with the issue of justice. Early Christians saw people like Dives die who never were good to other people, never shared, never loved, never were open to the Lord, and they struggled with the question: "How is justice done? If not here, then later?" They solved their problem of justice in a crass materialistic way. They sent him to Hades and made it into a place of eternal torture (a new concept, meant as a pedagogical tool, but with disastrous historical implications about the nature of God). They thought that God's justice could be achieved by burning people's behinds (Do they even have behinds to burn?). As preposterous as the image is, I'll bet 90 percent of Christians still believe literally in the flames of hell. They've accepted the mythological imagery that God's justice is somehow attained by people suffering physical pain. That's not what the Scriptures are teaching.

The Bible is simply saying, "Good is good, evil is evil. If you do what is good, you enjoy the fruits of the good. If you do what is evil, you will suffer evil." Let me repeat: The kingdom of God does not begin after a person dies; it is beginning right now. Therefore, it's heaven all the way to heaven, and it's hell all the way to hell. Heaven is primarily now, but that's not to deny it's life forever; and hell is primarily now, but that's not to deny it's death forever. Heaven and hell are states of being. Hell is the state of being where you don't love any more; it is to be cut off, to be alone, to be dead/without life.

The meaning of the teaching here is that if you choose death, you will in fact be dead. Lifelessness is to be in Hades, Sheol. It is nonlife, nonexistence. There are people who are dead already now. They may be walking around in bodies, but they are dead inside. They've permanently chosen nonlife, which we have named "hell." And hell is a possible choice (although we have never declared anybody to certainly be there). God is now offering you life, saying, "Live in the kingdom.

Choose life. Choose love. Choose sharing. Choose communion. They last forever." We call that forever "heaven" (and we have declared tens of thousands to certainly be there. We call them saints).

There are three things that last: faith, hope, and love. The gospel puts the decision before you. Buy into the real. Buy into the good forever. To surrender to the good is the choice for the kingdom. It is to surrender to what is eternal. If the Lord can bring about the call to the good in you only by threatening you with fire for all eternity, then in fact you have not chosen the good. That's not *you* freely choosing it. If you're going to church only as fire insurance, then you are still living in fear and not in its opposite, faith.

That spirit of fear, however, is what we're dealing with in the church today. We are often looking at "baptized pagans" who have not joined any voluntary faith community. Many people have not consciously chosen the good; many do not believe that the good is, in fact, good. They're coming to church involuntarily, under the law, and in fear of pain. You will never create the kingdom of God by law, fire, or fear.

The kingdom of God is created in freedom. And God is the one who totally respects your freedom. If the Bible isn't saying that, I don't know where else to begin. We have to return to a gospel of grace and freedom, which creates a people with dignity, life, and an ability to give, and not merely people going through cultural practices out of fear. There's nothing life-giving in that, and we don't need it any more. It's more the problem than the solution. God doesn't need it to get God's work done. And it doesn't liberate the human heart or anything else. There *is*, as Abraham says in the story (v. 26), a "great chasm" between heaven and hell — between fear and faith, between death and life. This lovely story was meant to help us overcome the chasm, but unfortunately has largely been used to deepen it.

Luke 17

Chapter 17 is on leading others astray, and it begins with warnings about creating "obstacles" for people who possess a simple faith. We must have good theology because there is so much sick religion and manipulative use of religion by toxic people. Good theology actually protects those whom Jesus calls "the little ones": "It would be better to have a millstone tied around your neck and be thrown into the sea" than for you to destroy the simple faith of people who love and trust God and others (see Luke 17:1–3). "Don't fix it if it's not broken," he says, but now he will balance it with, "If it *is* broken, do what you can to repair and mend."

Jesus also calls us to confrontation and correction. *"If your brother does something wrong, reprove him. If he is sorry, forgive him. And if he wrongs you seven times a day, and seven times come back to you, and says 'I'm sorry,' you must forgive him"* (17:3–4). So not only is Luke presenting a teaching on forgiveness, he is also admitting the existence of failure in the Christian community.

In the first days of the Charismatic Renewal, many of us idealistically thought, "Now I'm with Spirit-filled people and they'll all be totally committed to Jesus from now on." And we were sadly mistaken. I remember how disillusioned I was when I went to the seminary and met all these men in the seminary who didn't seem to love Jesus. I wondered, "Why are they here?"

But Luke is presuming failure in the Christian community. Even with all the best intentions in the world, given our different temperaments, backgrounds, and the way we process our data and information, we are going to step on one another's toes. Two people with absolutely good will can deeply hurt one another. Please acknowledge that. You may think that it's unimportant, but good people hurt one another because we all come at reality in different ways. That's why, for Jesus, the only way to achieve union is through forgiveness, not through making sin impossible or excommunicating nonconformists.

We would think the only way to achieve union is to gather together a group of absolutely good and healed people. No. Truth is deeper than that. Jesus says the only way to achieve union is through failure, vulnerability, and repair because people are always going to hurt one another. I wish authors would write realistically about lives of the saints, so we'd know that. We'd know that until the day they died, they had been doing things at which you and I would be scandalized. Medieval hagiographers selected only the data and legends they thought would appeal and inspire Christians of their day. In their own way they were trying to encourage virtue, but it was not as cleverly done as the evangelists did it. Nobody in the Bible, not even Jesus and Mary, would pass the strange litmus tests for holiness instituted later. The Bible presents real people who make real mistakes and work through them with God's help. (For example, both Moses and St. Paul were known murderers!)

You are on the same forgiveness path as the saints. The same Spirit is at work freeing you, you are struggling with the same difficulties they had, and you are learning both to receive and grant a universal forgiveness. I think it is the sum and substance of Jesus' teaching — and Luke's Gospel. If you don't "get" forgiveness, you don't get the core message.

"The apostles said to the Lord, 'Increase our faith' " (17:5). It's interesting that this request is put right after Jesus' teaching on forgiveness. They're saying, "How can we do that? How can we possibly forgive someone seventy-times-seven times? Increase our faith."

He replied, "All you need is a little bit of faith: *"If you had faith the size of a mustard seed, you could say to this mulberry tree, 'Be uprooted and planted in the sea,' and it would obey you"* (17:6). Jesus is not trying to create a circus of amazing events. He's trying to create faith on earth, that's all. He's not trying to get us to accomplish astounding feats, so everybody goes "Oooooh." Impressive stunts don't mean anything. The flying mulberry tree is an image to tell you of the power of faith, its power to achieve the impossible, in this case forgiveness of offending "brothers."

This is, of course, the second time Luke has spoken of a mustard seed (see 13:18). It's meaning there is clear — something small that slowly grows and has much larger effects.

"Asked by the Pharisees when the kingdom of God was to come, he gave them this answer. 'The kingdom of God does not admit of observation' " (17:20). The Pharisees are determined to force the kingdom into parameters and perimeters. They want to be able to say, "Those inside our system are in, those outside are out of it." The churches still do that. What a waster of time and wisdom.

"There will be no one to say, 'Look here! Look there!' For you must know the kingdom of God is among you" (17:21). We're never going to have the luxury of verification by observation, saying, "Those within this church are in the kingdom of God. The 144,000 elect, referred to in Revelations 7:4, belong to our denomination." Every church wants to claim they are coterminous with the kingdom. No visible institution will ever be the same as God's work on earth.

He told us very clearly right here, "Give it up." Let go of that need to divide the world into the righteous and the unrighteous. *"For you must know, the kingdom of God is among you"* (17:21). It is scattered out, it is shared, it is quiet, it is at work, it is powerful. But it's never going to be subject to neat and quick separation, e.g., those who celebrate this sacramental system are in, those who obey the Ten Commandments are in, those who are baptized by immersion are in. Every church has its own quality control system for getting into the kingdom, because we're all playing the same game that Judaism played. Why not just love God and your neighbor and leave everything else up to God? Maybe that is why the text now becomes final and apocalyptic.

This short teaching on the last days (17:22–37) is why the most recent biblical scholars conclude that Luke's book is written around the year 85, because he doesn't seem to be applying this teaching to the fall of Jerusalem, which happened in 70. He's applying it to the *end of time.* "Don't try to predict the final day. Don't try to say how or when it's going to happen. The Lord will come when he will." This was to free us from preoccupation with the end times, but has not had much success with some groups.

Luke 18

Chapter 18 presents two stories on prayer: the insistent widow (18:2–8) and the Pharisee and the publican (18:9–14). Since we have already talked about perseverance in prayer, let's look at the second story. This latter is another one of those stories that I'd be afraid to create myself. Imagine if I got up in a Catholic suburban parish and said, "A man came to me who is a member of the Knights of Columbus and the St. Vincent de Paul Society, sends his children to a Catholic school, is faithful to his wife, pays all his bills on time, and lives right down the street from you in middle America. Then there's another man, who isn't doing any of these things; in fact, he's a corrupt tax collector, a loser, a failure in every sense. One day, these two men happened to come into the church at the same time. I'm telling you that this loser, this failure, this nothing person is deemed acceptable to God and the good guy is judged unworthy!" Can you imagine the icy silence I would feel? And how they would ask the bishop to reappoint me to some other parish as soon as possible?

Well, that's what Jesus is saying. "You people are missing what the kingdom is all about." This publican had the attitude of dependence, of trust in God. He knew who he was. The contemporary image of the publican for me is recovering alcoholics. They don't have any illusions about themselves as so many of us do. They know they're weak. They can use straightforward talk. They're like little children sometimes, so humble and good, but they're losers, the world would say. We're all losers, but most of us don't know it.

God isn't trying just to make us good; he's trying to make us truthful — and that's goodness. Our definition of goodness is largely something covering up something else. Humility and honesty are the predictable qualities of truly good people. God has not called us to success it seems; God has called us to surrender.

Healing Touch

Immediately after that, Jesus has them bring the children to him. Here you can see Luke's associational mind working. The image of the little child seems to be a continuation of the simple tax collector we have just met. He has nothing to give; like a child he can only receive. *"People even brought little children to him, for him to touch them; but when the disciples saw this, they turned them away. But Jesus called the children to him and said, 'Let the little children come to me and do not stop them, for it is to such as these that the kingdom of God belongs'"* (18:15–17). Note that Jesus does not teach them. He only notices them, values them, and "touches" them.

When I was down in St. Lucia in the West Indies, I noticed that in great part the fathers there do not raise their children. It is a task solely for mothers. Of course, we white folks have ourselves to blame for that. We destroyed the black family through slavery, putting men in one plantation, women and children in another. For two or three generations, black men never saw their families. We realize today how we — whites as well as blacks — are still suffering from that sin, that evil of slavery, what we did to a whole race. The white people talk about "those terrible blacks," not being faithful, etc. But who is finally to blame? Before white people made them slaves, they had as beautiful a family unit as any we have.

On this whole island, there are very few faithful fathers and husbands, so the women raise the children and have a world all their own. Beautiful mothers, some with a dozen children around them, don't expect the fathers to help. The women have taken the whole job on themselves. We see this in America too. Black mothers have had to play the roles of both parents — and have risen to the occasion.

On the island, little boys never get any kind of affirmation from an adult male; men there largely ignore children. We sent two young men from New Jerusalem Community to work down there for a year. They said if you were walking through the street and showed any sign of affirmation to a boy, like running your hands through a little boy's hair and smiling at him, he'd probably do anything for you, even jump off a cliff if you asked him to. One of our young men said, "We'd talk to the children, and adults would stop and watch us: a *man* bothering to talk to children."

So when I was there, I went out among the crowds and walked the streets with the young boys. They were all Catholic, so there was a deep faith expectancy there already, and they loved the religious habit. All I'd have to do would be to put my hand on one of their heads or squeeze their arms and, honestly, within a few minutes children would be surrounding me, four deep — just waiting. They never tired of the recognition. They were so innocent, just waiting for some man to affirm them and show some sign of caring and blessing. That's what Jesus is doing here.

Don't forget the power of touch — the nonverbal is far more sacramental than words. On the one hand, we are so afraid of the dangers and excesses of physical expression, but on the other hand everything about our nature tells us that's where life is most deeply communicated. Jesus clearly understood.

Danger of Riches

Soon Luke is back to haranguing rich people again. "*A member of one of the leading families put this question to him. 'Good Master, what must I do to have a life that is eternal?'* " (18:18–19). Notice how Jesus ignores the flattery and points beyond himself to God. "*Why do you call me good? God is good*" (18:19).

This is one of those passages that we often just slough over and for-get. Jesus very obviously sees a distinction between himself and God. "That's God, the one who alone is good. I'm Jesus." This is his human self-consciousness at work. "God is the source of goodness. I'm God's instrument. I know God's using me. I'm God's prophet. I want to be God's son."

He says, " '*You know the commandments.*' . . . *The man replied,*

'I've kept all these from my earliest days till now.' When Jesus heard this, he said, 'There is still one thing you lack. Sell all that you own and distribute the money to the poor, and you'll have treasure in heaven. Then come and follow me.' But when he heard this, he was filled with sadness, for he was very rich" (18:18–23). Don't ever think that the kingdom is an all-or-nothing situation. The Lord doesn't say, "If that's your reaction, you're damned and going to hell." He's simply saying, "If you really want to enter into the freedom I'm talking about, if you want a life that is forever, if you want to enter into the really real, then since you asked me the question, I'm going to give you an answer. Give it away. It will possess you more than you will ever possess it." The man says, "Well, I just can't do that right now." And Jesus replies, "Okay. You asked, I answered."

Unlike Jesus' reply, some would reply to the rich man by making Jesus' recommendation a law. They would say, "You have to do it." Jesus says, in effect, "I'm not trying to make a law out of what I said, but if you want to know the goal of the kingdom, if you want to experience the ideal of freedom God is talking about, there it is. Sell all that you own and distribute the money to the poor."

Our contemporary dangerous tendency toward most of the economic statements made in the New Testament has not been to make a law out of them (although we did it with sexual issues), but to completely ignore them — pretend that they're not there at all.

In the next passage (18:24–27), Luke continues, *"Jesus looked at him and said, 'How hard it is for those who have riches to make their way into the kingdom of God'"* (18:24). Among the Jewish people of Jesus' day, wealth was thought of as a sign of God's blessing. Jesus simply says that is not true. Wealth is not a sign of God's blessing. How many give testimonies of God's blessings today and are saying basically, "Because God made me wealthy, it shows God loves me. God made this business deal work."

The Lord is saying that is not true. *"It is easier for a camel to pass through the eye of a needle than for a rich man to enter the kingdom of God"* (18:25). The listeners are shocked by this. To show it's a shocking statement, they ask, "In that case, who can be saved?" (v. 26) They recognize they all have money and there was no exegete there telling them that the "eye of a needle" was a small but manageable gate in the walls of the city!

Jesus tells them not to make a law out of it again by explaining,

"Things that are impossible for men are possible with God" (18:26–27). In other words, says Jesus, "It's God's problem. Salvation is God's problem. I'm giving you the gospel of freedom, the gospel of peace. Live it as best you can and leave the problem of salvation up to God. Don't start evaluating who is saved and who isn't. That is not your problem. Simply proclaim the good news of the kingdom."

The Quality of Faith

The account of the man born blind (18:35–43) is an interesting example of an oral tradition, because we find it told by each of the four evangelists. The story is used somewhat differently in each of the gospels. Luke has Jesus entering the city of Jericho (18:35), Matthew and Mark have him coming out of the city of Jericho (Matt. 20:29; Mark 10:46). Each evangelist uses the city and the story for his own purpose. Mark names the blind man Bartimeus; Luke gives him no name, Matthew has two blind men. In John 9, the cure of the blind man might well be part of the same oral tradition, and John tells a very long story. If you are honest with the text, you will notice how different the effect the same story has in each account. This kind of textual comparison helps us come to understand how there was an oral tradition out of which came the written gospels.

Luke emphasizes the beautiful faith relationship beginning between Jesus and the blind man. *"He called out, 'Son of David, have pity on me.' Jesus stopped and ordered them to bring the man to him. And when he came up, Jesus asked him, 'What do you want me to do for you?' He said, 'Sir, let me see again.' And Jesus said, 'Receive your sight, your faith has saved you' "* (18:39–43). It is important to recognize the role of faith and the faith relationship at work here.

What does having faith or trusting in God mean? Trusting is not a passive dependency, a handing over of responsibility, that says, "Okay, God, you can do it." Faith in God is primarily an active virtue, not a passive one. Faith does not necessarily mean or expect that God will intervene. Faith is an end in itself. *Faith is an active empowering of the other to be everything he or she can be for you.* It calls forth in the other and in oneself what it sees. Some would simply call it "the power of positive thinking" or self-fulfilling trust.

Those who are parents can probably relate to this definition. That little baby you were holding looked up at you with total faith and expectation. It had faith in you. You became a mother because the child made you into a mother; the child actively empowered you to be everything you could be for it. Between the years when your children were one and six, you became capable of almost totally losing yourself in them. It's unbelievable what mothers go through, running constantly all day. Would you ever have thought you could lose yourself that way? You did it because you were the object of your child's faith. Only a child's faith in you and a child's need of you could bring that incredible power and dedication out of a human being.

The faith of the blind man, saying, "Jesus, I need you, I love you, I want you," becomes the channel of trust and openness through which the power of Jesus can flow to heal that person and change that person's life. I think this is one of the most central things about faith that I can say. It is a *quality of relationship* which works "magic," although Jesus resists any attempt to be seen or used as a magician.

I repeat, faith is an end in itself. It is not a means to something further. Faith is not what we do in order to get into heaven. Mutual perfect faith would *be* heaven! Faith is its own end. To have faith is already to have come alive. "Your faith has saved you," (18:42) is the way Jesus put it to the blind man.

Faith is the opposite of resentment, cynicism and negativity. Faith is always, finally, a self-fulfilling prophecy. Faith actually begins to create what it desires. Faith always re-creates the good world. Without faith, we all sink into the bad world that we most feared. With faith, you keep trusting, hoping, believing and calling forth life from stones, which is exactly what Jesus intimates in the next chapter (19:40). You can call life forth from anything if you already possess life. You can make a stone breathe, make it live for you, make it shout out in praise of God. As has been so often said, faith is a matter of having new eyes, seeing everything through and even with the eyes of God.

Luke 19

Zacchaeus is the tax collector who knew he needed God's mercy (see Luke 18:13–14). Although Zacchaeus is a short man, he is also wealthy. And although it is difficult for a rich man to enter the kingdom, he is an example of "nothing is impossible to God." Although he is a senior tax collector, he is also humble. In climbing up a tree, he showed he was willing to make a fool of himself just to see what kind of man Jesus was.

Zacchaeus expects much from the Lord, so the Lord expects much from him. Zacchaeus is ready to do all that the Lord expects. Luke has him saying, *"I'm willing to give half my property to the poor and if I have cheated anybody, I will pay him back four times the amount"* (19:8). Now there's a free and generous heart. Jesus seems to praise him because he is wealthy but not greedy or oppressive of the poor.

We can read this entire gospel on two levels simultaneously. To those who are handicapped, little, and poor, Jesus is always saying, in effect, "Come up!" To those who are rich and comfortable like Zacchaeus, he inevitably says, "Come down!" (v. 5), which is exactly what Zacchaeus does. He is, in fact, the only clear example of the same. No wonder Jesus is so pleasantly surprised and even goes to his house for dinner.

The parable of the pounds in chapter 19 is treated at length in my book *Simplicity* (Crossroad, 1992, chapter 9). For me it is a central example of reading a text from the outside and getting an entirely fresh and credible interpretation. In this case, modern historical research also allows the radical interpretation, where the one we thought to be the hero is really the villain, and the so-called loser is really the civil-disobedient hero.

If you don't like this interpretation, try: *Share it or lose it.* Those who simply keep hoarding what they have will end up losing everything. To those who use what they have, invest it, and share it, God gives more. They, in fact, Jesus says, become the truly wealthy ones (19:26). Remember, there is never one and only one interpretation to a sacred text.

Five

Jerusalem, Passion, Death, Resurrection

Luke 19, 20, 21

In the last segment of chapter 19, Jesus enters Jerusalem. The allusion here is to Zechariah 9:9: "Rejoice heart and soul, daughter of Sion! Shout with gladness, daughter of Jerusalem! See now, your king comes to you; he is victorious, he is triumphant, humble and riding on a donkey, on a colt, the foal of a donkey" (Zech. 9:9).

Luke used that image as he has Jesus entering the Holy City. He's coming into charge of his possession, namely, his people; and Luke has him coming in, according to the prophecy, as the Messiah. He is a humble Messiah, inaugurating a new kind of Messiahship, not one controlled by power but one brought about by servanthood. He's riding a donkey, an animal of humility.

As Jesus is coming into Jerusalem, *"the whole group of disciples joyfully begin to praise God at the top of their voices for the miracles they had seen"* (19:37). Some of the Pharisees said, "Check your disciples, they're too turned on, too charismatic. Cool them down; they've got to act respectfully."

He said, "I tell you, if these keep silent, the very stones will cry out" (19:39–40). An interesting juxtaposition of intense emotion in two directions. Actually it is easy to imagine how the one would follow from the other. Such needed joy — denied and condemned — could only become tears, the tears of missed opportunity, as we see in verse 44. Then he cries over the city of Jerusalem. He sheds tears (19:41).

He enters the temple and drives out the dealers who were selling things there (19:45–46). He's taking over the temple because he is to *reimage* the temple in himself. He begins to teach there "every day" (v. 44), and this is surely the historical action that finally gets him killed. Here he takes on the entire lie of false religion: temple taxes, purity and debt codes, the primacy of "sacrifices" over mercy and compassion.

Up until this time in Luke, Jesus' controversies have been largely with Pharisees over issues having to do with legalism. Now in these last chapters, when he comes into the city, his controversies are with the priests and the scribes — the establishment. The issues are now questions of authority. *"He taught in the temple every day. The chief priests and scribes tried to do away with him. But they did not see how they could carry this out because the people hung on his words"* (19:47–48).

Luke 20

The priests and scribes questioned his authority (20:1–8) then they tried to trap him theologically, regarding paying taxes to Caesar (20:20–26). Usually Jesus will not be led into a theological trap when he can see they are just playing games. Instead, he sidesteps their trap and presents them with an image or tells a story.

I think Jesus' way of responding is important to notice, because of how common religious debate is today. Contemporary people like to argue theologically. For example, religious people who come to your door like to challenge you about Scripture passages. Luke's point is that arguing and debating about Scripture and theology is not faith-building. It goes nowhere. According to Luke, the method of Jesus is to bypass theological traps. He knows when he is being manipulated. He does not give himself to manipulation and showmanship. That approach does not appeal to him, so he will speak a quiet but powerful truth and let it stand there. Often he will ask a question in return instead of answering theirs, as he does here in verses 24–25.

Controversy undermines real faith because it destroys relationships and respect between people. In such discussions, people feel on the defensive or offensive. They don't experience a safe atmosphere of love, but rather a competitive game where battling egos take the place of God's truth — which is always relational.

Again and again, Jesus has hard words for the scribes. *"Beware of the scribes who like to walk around in long robes, who love to be greeted in the marketplace, to take the front seats in synagogues, who swallow the property of widows. The more severe will be their sentence"* (20:46–47). I would be afraid to say that at a clergy convention, but one time it was the assigned reading of the day, and I preached on it in my long robe and from the front seat!

Luke 21

Luke next tells the story of the widow's mite (21:1–4), again turning upside down the value systems of the world. God isn't interested in how much you give, but in why you give. God doesn't look at the amount of the gift, but at the spirit of the giver. It also follows, intentionally I am sure, from the previous sentence about "swallowing the property of widows." We are supposed to be able to conclude *why* she is so poor. (Let the reader beware of seemingly innocent passages.)

Luke presents Jesus' discourse on the destruction of Jerusalem. By the time Luke is writing his gospel, the destruction of Jerusalem and the temple has probably already happened, so for Luke's readers the discourse is not so much a prophesy as it is a historic description. The event has already happened. The great city has been destroyed.

Luke puts this discourse into his narrative because he's saying, in effect, "It doesn't matter at all. The destruction of the Holy City is nothing catastrophic for us, because Jesus is now Jerusalem. For us, Jesus is the temple, and the New City." All self-serving religion must eventually die. Remember that a Jew's shock at this would surpass a Catholic's dismay if the Vatican were destroyed.

Look at this verse: *"Take care not to be deceived. Many will come, using my name and saying 'I am he' and 'The time is near at hand.' Refuse to join them"* (21:8). These are the "end time singers." We still hear them today. Jesus is telling us right there, "When you hear them chanting, 'The time is near,' refuse to join them. And when you hear of wars and revolutions, do not be afraid. Of course they're going to happen, but don't orient your whole life around a fear of great wars and revolutions. They are something that must happen, but the end is not so soon."

The call of the Lord is always to live in the present. Suppose we knew for certain the date that the world was going to end. What would we do differently, except, I hope, to continue what we are already doing.

If the only way we can motivate our people to live a life of goodness is to talk about end times, then they are not motivated at all. If people are following the Lord only because the world is going to end, then they're not really following the Lord. They're simply trying to avoid disaster. We need lovers, delighters, positive builders — not dour naysayers. Much of chapter 21 is a continuation of that theme — the time of his coming.

To assert that the world is going to end is not morbid teaching; it's realistic. To live as if your life is not going to end is to live a lie. To pretend that life will go on forever is precisely that, a pretense. By the year 2090, none of us will be walking this earth any more. We're not going to be here. What does that mean? We'll all be has-beens. Some of us will be talked about, but most of us will be forgotten. We're sitting here alive now, but soon we'll be all gone. It keeps us not only from taking ourselves too seriously, but it also helps us to take ourselves *very seriously.*. That's why the gospel was always presented in that tension of the end time.

That paradoxical polarity is an important point in teaching of the end times and I don't want to ignore it. We live in the specter of our own personal end times. You and I are going to die. Every primitive initiation rite felt it had to communicate that to the young teenager. The symbolic drowning of baptism was supposed to do the same. Now it is the books on life-after-death experiences — or real death experiences — that teach the same needed truth.

When your whole life passes before you, no single thing is really that important. In other words, don't sell your soul for winning one little argument or resolving one little situation or overcoming one little pain — don't let that single moment, no matter how important it may seem to you now, control the rest of your life. Some might be still suffering from a rejection they experienced twenty years ago and they let this one event control their whole life.

When you realize that everything is important, and yet it is all passing away, then no individual event matters that much. *You can let it go* — which is what Jesus himself now has to do. Note that we speak of this as his "passion" (that which is suffered, allowed, endured, done *to you*) and not as his action (that which we choose and perhaps control). It is, finally, his passion which liberates and redeems him and us, even more than his action.

Luke 22 and 23

Chapter 22 begins the Passion, which includes the conspiracy, the betrayal, the preparation for the Passover supper, and the supper itself. The story Luke tells is not very different from the other synoptic gospels. We're all familiar with it.

If we want to look for a ritualized myth of the life of Jesus, it's the Last Supper. Because it sums up his life it became the central sacrament and liturgy of our church. The Last Supper event is the central means by which we create church. On the night before he died, he gathered his beloved around him and they experienced the sharing of life and the sharing of death together. That supper event is the Jesus myth summarized in ritual form.

To experience the full depth of meaning of the Lord's Supper is to somehow experience the essence of Christianity, its life of sharing and communion, its life of surrender and faith. Eucharist is so powerful! If only the church fully understood the gift it has.

Once again, it's important to mention that the Eucharist is not just a gift for gaining points with God, which is what so many people have made it into. We are so self-focused and concerned about our own security that we miss the meaning of the life-and-death banquet. (Every Mass has the same theme — the paschal mystery.)

Eucharist is not only the sacrament that defines church, it is also the celebration that creates church and continues to lead the "faithful assembled" on their journey.

Catholics are very lucky because not every Christian denomination enjoys this gift of Eucharist. Because we in the New Jerusalem Community are a Catholic community, we're also a eucharistic community. What holds together New Jerusalem, our small faith community in Cincinnati, is Eucharist. (In 1997, I would now say the same about the Center for Action and Contemplation in Albuquerque.) When a group is held together by the nonverbal language of Eucharist, it can absorb a wide spectrum of differentiation. Our community's members are held together by eating of the same bread and drinking of the same cup, not by all saying the same words. If you don't have Eucharist holding a faith community together, what do you have to give it cohesion? A preacher with words? Then the question becomes, "Do you like the preacher, what he says and how he interprets Scripture?"

Any Catholic community is held together not by preachers, but by

Eucharist. The celebration of Eucharist together happens in nonverbal language, which is much broader, deeper and more catholic — universal — than verbal preacher-language. As a preacher, the way I talk is bound to turn off a certain number of people. Probably a lot. Many don't want to think the way I do or say things my way. When you remove the altar from the center of the Christian community, what's left to put in its place is the pulpit. Then the only way you can unite people is to see if they agree on your scriptural translation, interpretation, and emphasis.

We Catholics haven't heard many great preachers in our lives. We don't come to church because the celebrant preaches great sermons. We know that the sermon may be second-rate, and we've accepted that years ago. We don't expect great sermons. Maybe that's unfortunate. I'm not saying it should be that way, but the quality of the sermon is not what holds us together. It's Eucharist that creates the bond holding us together. We eat the body of the Lord and we drink the blood of the Lord. In this way we become one flesh. There is deep wisdom in that. That's the power of catholicity — to be able to absorb nineteen different rites in the church. I hope someday we have 150 different rites in the church — the Methodist rite, the Presbyterian rite, the Pentecostal rite. Then the church will be truly catholic.

Right after the apostles have experienced the Eucharist, Luke presents them arguing among themselves about "who is the greatest?" What irony and yet what genius in the placing of this story here!

"A dispute arose among them about which should be reckoned the greatest. Jesus said, 'That's the way pagans think. Among pagans it is the kings who lord it over them. No, this must not happen among you. The greatest among you must behave as if you were the youngest, the leader as if he were the one who serves'" (22:24–26). That is probably the simplest and most powerful statement about the Christian definition of authority to be found in all four gospels.

"For who is the greater, the one at table or the one who serves?" The world would say immediately, "The one at table." He says, *"Surely, yet, here I am among you as one who serves"* (22:27). Jesus says, in effect, "I'm telling you that the world's way will not work. The essence of true freedom is the freedom to serve other people — to wait upon them."

What in fact happened historically in our church, growing so much out of the European medieval situation, was that ministry in the church came to be identified with power and hierarchy because our church leaders modeled themselves on the princes and lords of Europe. Recently I visited several bishops' "pleasure palaces" in Salzburg. It amazes me that the Austrians are still Catholic after so many centuries of blatant gospel abuse.

Christianity sold out to the world's model of authority. The church said, "If a king has a crown, then the pope is three times better; he has to have a tiara, three crowns in one." I'm not saying it's wrong as such for the pope to wear a tiara, but, historically speaking, that image came from medieval hierarchical thinking, and I'm not going to take it too seriously. Jesus wore a crown of thorns, not a tiara.

We might wonder, "How did that happen?" This is one reason for learning our history. I hope I've learned enough to give me some patience so that I don't condemn the past and say they were all wrong and stupid. The medieval ecclesiastical leaders were trying to say that the church is better than the state, the kingdom of God is more important than the kingdom of this world. Now that's true. But, unfortunately, in trying to express that truth they sold out to the symbol system of the world.

If the king could have a train on his robe that was fifty feet long, then a cardinal was allowed to have a train fifty-five feet long. Suddenly in church processions cardinals begin to have satin trains with ermine on them because the church is greater than the state. On one level, you can acknowledge their assumptions, but on the level that matters, it was *behavioral heresy* by those who call themselves the teachers ("magisterium"). It was only at Vatican II that much wearing of outrageous vestments stopped. Now it is hard to believe that anyone would want to wear such stuff.

As a result, we're once again struggling to redefine authority in the church. Long ago, church ministry became "office" rather than function. The priesthood is still infected with that power of position, since priesthood is still seen as an office — a role given to a person that metaphysically raises him above everybody else in the believing community. The priest is in that office forever, says the church. But the real ministry question to the priest is: "Are you really functioning as the one who elicits the act of faith from people, who creates God's community?" Are you an "agent of transformation" for the soul or merely for bread?

Thank God, we Catholics are returning to an emphasis on function and service rather than office, but we're just in the beginning stages of understanding the true source of authority in the church. Jesus clearly says that authority comes from living the life of servanthood, from being involved in serving others and laying down your life for the brothers and sisters. You deserve to be called a priest or minister in the church not simply because you have a title or wear a priestly garb but because you've laid down your life for the community. Gospel authority comes from living the paschal mystery, not from having hands laid on you. What should flow from the laying on the hands is people empowered to lay down their lives for the Body of Christ.

In our current system, you get ordained because basically you earned passing grades in philosophy and theology courses over many years. It is possible, on the day you are ordained, that you have never elicited the act of faith from a single person. You've never had to be involved in real ministry, just pass tests. Then, one day they lay hands on you and you're called a priest. Frankly, a lot of priests don't know how to do ministry, don't know how to talk to people or relate to them. Many priests are not sure of their own faith, so how can they know how to evoke it from others?

Sometimes seminarians haven't even lived a community life. Many have lived in solitary little rooms as students for nine years. Then, suddenly, they're supposed to be a communitarian person building a community of faith. The fact is, frankly, on ordination day many of us were afraid of community. How can it be that priests are afraid of people — of women, of children — yet are supposed to call them together to be the people of God? Can you see the practical problems we're up against in ministry?

For Jesus, authority comes from servanthood. I'm not denying the efficacy of the sacrament of ordination but merely asking, as Luke did, "Where does the true power come from?" Is it merely "from above," an objective gift (symbolized in the laying on of hands), or is it not also "from below," a subjective transformation of the self (in servanthood)? The second "ordination" seems to be the more important, and many lay people have it more than many formally ordained.

Jesus says, *"You are the men who have stood faithfully by me in my trials"* (22:28). This is Jesus' criterion for priestly ministry. *"So now I confer on you a kingdom"* (22:29), *"just as my father conferred one on me. You will eat and drink at my table in my kingdom, and you will sit on thrones to judge the twelve tribes of Israel"* (22:30).

The future church took those "thrones" too literally and began to believe that ruling over others is really what the kingdom is about. Jesus is establishing clear criteria here. He is pointing out what qualifies a person for sitting on a throne and being a judge and leader of God's people. It is to *"stand by me, faithfully in my trial"* (22:28). This means, in effect, "To walk the journey of faith with me, go through the Exodus with me, suffer and die with me.

"Simon, Simon! Satan, you know, has got his wish to sift you all like wheat; but I prayed for you, Simon, that your faith may not fail, and once you have recovered, you in your turn must strengthen your brothers" (22:31–32). Note that the precise prayer for Peter is that (1) "his *faith* not fail" and (2) "once you have recovered" — which implies a Jonah-in-the-whale testing, and (3) "You must strengthen your brothers."

I believe that much of our disappointment and disillusionment with the vicar of Peter, the pope, in history is that we expected too much from him (e.g., love and hope). All Jesus prays for is that he hold us together in *faith*, by first going through the trials of faith himself. Once I saw and understood this passage, I became much more patient and modest in my expectations.

During Jesus' arrest, denial, and mockery, Luke has Jesus constantly being proclaimed innocent. Herod and Pilate both say he is innocent (23:4, 11–12). Luke wants us to know it's the innocent Jesus being murdered.

Jesus is the archetypal scapegoat, the symbolic victim that we all create to exonerate ourselves (see Lev. 16). When the victim of Rome and Jerusalem is subsequently proclaimed the Lord of History, we have released an empathy for the victim and a radical critique of all glorified violence (see *Violence Unveiled* by Gil Bailie [Crossroad, 1995], a pivotal and very important book!).

During the crucifixion scene, Luke tells the story of the Good Thief. Luke uses this chance to emphasize again the theme of the merciful Jesus. Merciful and universally accepting until the very end, Luke's Jesus is ready for all. To this thief who has led an evil life, supposedly, Jesus says, *"Indeed, I promise you today you will be with me in paradise"* (23:43).

Through the centuries, that generous burst of forgiveness from Jesus in the last moment has given hope to many people. In that scene with the good thief, Luke reminds us once again that salvation is not earned or bought by our doing good works; it is the result of a love-trust relationship wherein God's life can be communicated to us.

The game of earning, worthiness, tit-for-tat, sacrifices of atonement is over. "Go learn the meaning of the phrase, 'What I want is mercy, not your sacrifices'" (Hos. 6:6).

People's final words are often used to summarize the meaning of their whole life. Luke presents Jesus' final words as: *"Father, into your hands I commit my spirit"* (23:46). There, in one line, is the meaning of Jesus' spirituality: he trusted in the Father and was not put to shame. He trusted in the Father's faithful love; he believed against all odds that the Father was Father (so perfectly a "father," in fact, that God was very much a mother!). Against all evidence to the contrary, he believed God was faithful. And he stated that belief in his very last breath.

So the pattern we are about to see completed in the Easter story has really in fact already happened on the cross. Jesus has already made the "great Passover." He is free, enlightened, saved, and in the hands of God. Now he becomes both our promise and our pattern — revealed in one whole life.

Luke 24

God's miracle in Jesus is not the resurrection as we've made it out to be. Is God able to raise up a body that has died? Of course God can do that. If God is God, of course God can raise up a body. The resurrection of Jesus' body is no big miracle. The unbelievable word of faith that should be spoken to all of us in the Easter story is what the Spirit of God achieved in the heart of Jesus: that the Spirit liberated Jesus' heart so he could let go of himself to God. Even though he did flinch, have questions, and feel doubt, he still remained faithful. That's the Easter miracle achieved in the humanity of Jesus.

That miracle of liberation receives a symbolic but real expression in the raising up of his body on Easter Sunday morning. It tells us he is whole, he is for real, he is the true God-man, the one who holds together heaven and earth. He is the synthesis who is totally of this world and yet gave himself totally to the Father.

For all time he becomes our sign, our promise, our guarantee, our fulfillment. It's all summed up in Jesus: He's the beginning, the middle, and the end. For us, he is everything. He is the Word of the Father. He is what God can accomplish in humanity when we say yes to God.

This insight about the resurrection has not commonly been taught. Traditionally, we were told the resurrection was the proof that Jesus was really God. Now to say that God is really Love is different from saying that the resurrection proves that Jesus was really God.

As I said in the beginning, the first faith question that every person is asking is not:. "Is Jesus God?" but "Can God be trusted?" or "Is God for us?" The resurrection is saying, "Yes, God can be trusted. God is turning our crucifixions into life."

In Luke's final chapter the resurrection is a given. It has happened. On the first day of the week they come looking for him. Notice it is the women coming. Faithful to the end, the women are the ones who listen to the Lord. Luke doesn't have the disciples coming to the tomb; none of them go looking, except Peter (24:12). It was the women who first believed.

"As they stood there not knowing what to think, two men in bril-liant clothes suddenly appeared at their side. Terrified, the women lowered their eyes" (24:5). Again, the experience of the Holy evokes a response of reverence and awe. *"The two men said, 'Why look among the dead for someone who is alive? He is not here; he is Risen. Remember what he told you when he was still in Galilee' "* (24:5–6).

"And they remembered his words" (24:8). So the women ran to the Eleven and to all the others (24:9). Luke names three of the women who went looking as "Mary of Magdala, Joanna, and Mary the mother of James" (24:10), but he doesn't mention Mary the mother of Jesus.

"The other women with them also told the apostles. But this story of theirs seemed pure nonsense, and they did not believe" (24:11). The first response recorded of the leaders of the church is nonbelief. At least Peter was curious. *"Peter, however, went running to the tomb. He bent down and saw the binding cloths, nothing else. He went back home amazed"* (24:12). Nothing else. No faith yet. So still the "offi-cial" church does not believe. For Luke, Peter always represents the church. The church is sometimes the last to believe the word of God. The women are the *anawim*, the little poor ones. Simple people can believe, but the official church and its leaders are slow to believe.

Then comes the beautiful account on the road to Emmaus. Scholars used to suppose that Luke himself was one of the two on the road. We don't know. To what degree it is based on historical fact, we don't know. It is not found in any of the other gospels.

It has those lines we all love so much, *"Did not our hearts burn within us"* (24:32) *"... and they knew him in the breaking of bread"* (24:35). In this story, Luke is teaching his community about Christ's presence among them. He hears them asking something like, "Okay, it's the year 80 already, we don't see Jesus any more, so how is Jesus present to us?" Luke's response is, "He's present in the breaking of the bread — the Eucharist." It's a very clear teaching on Eucharist.

"We know him in this celebration, in the ongoing appropriation of the story. We can't sit down at the table like the first disciples did. I wasn't there myself," Luke says, "but we can sit at a new table in our town and experience the Lord's Supper just as they did, and know him just as they did in the breaking of bread — and our hearts will burn within us."

Jesus finally appears to the Eleven. He showed them his hands and his feet. *"Why are you so agitated? Why do these doubts rise in your hearts?"* (23:38).

"Their joy was so great" (23:41). So their first response is joy — just at being with him again. It's not faith yet, just joy. *"They still could not believe it, and they stood there dumbfounded"* (23:41).

So he said to them, *"Have you anything to eat? And they offered him a piece of grilled fish, which he took and ate before their eyes"* (23:42–43). So he seems anxious to show that he is real, that he is embodied. This is the tenth and final meal setting in Luke's Gospel.

If we gather all the gospels together, we see that the teaching on the resurrection is not focused on the *physical resuscitation* of the body of Jesus. The resurrected body is a whole new type of corpo-reality, a new type of bodiliness which is open to universal presence and yet is immediately available to one person. Jesus has become the all-available Christ. Now that's the mystery we were taught back in our old catechism about the nature of the glorified body: it was bodi-liness and yet it was not bodiliness. It's still who you are now, yet very different.

At present, our human nature in its physical form is limited to a space-time continuum. My current body is a limited presence; if I'm here, I can't be there. That's not true of Jesus any more. What the gospels seem to be trying to say is that in the resurrection of the body we're getting into a new kind of bodiliness, a new kind of presence which is unlimited. Moreover, this limitless presence is a presence that is active and alive in each situation.

He gives them a final teaching (24:44–49), then he ascends. *"He took them out as far as the outskirts of Bethany and lifting up his hands, he blessed them"* (23:50). Blessing doesn't mean making a Sign of the Cross on them, as we think of it today. Blessing simply means praying over people, which we can all do.

"As he blessed them, he withdrew from them and was carried up into heaven. They worshiped him and they went back to Jerusalem full of joy; and they were continually in the temple, praising God" (23:51–53). In this last scene, Luke has created an image of the church. He's tying together his community with the apostles. He says, in effect, "Now you can recognize what we're doing when we pray together in our little community. This is where our liturgy all started. This joyful, spirit-filled group of people who knew the risen Jesus prayed together just as we do. That was the beginning of our tradition. You are now a part of it." Luke's Gospel ends in Jerusalem, where it began; his Acts of the Apostles will begin at that same point.

I hope my comments on Luke's Gospel give you the encouragement and faith to read all of the gospels in a fair and faith-filled way. My whole desire has been to build up and create faith in you. I'd be totally untrue to Luke's intention if I desired anything else. I want to expand, not limit, your reality of the Lord. I don't want to explain things away; I want to fill Luke's writings with meaning and life for you.

It is my concluding prayer that the Lord grant us all a deeper faith in Jesus through our brother Luke.